Immanuel

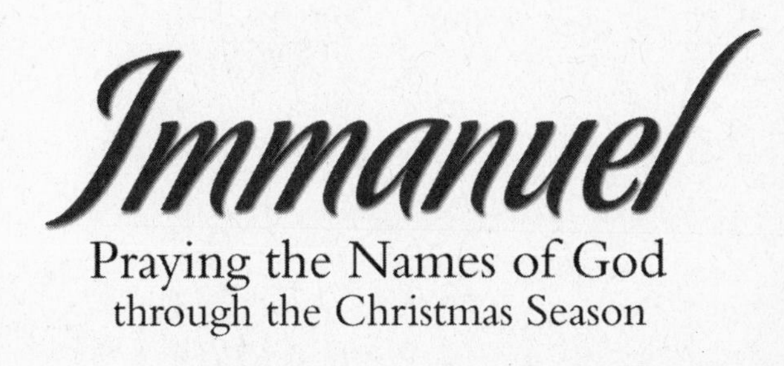

ANN SPANGLER

Immanuel

Requests for information should be addressed to:

Zondervan, *Grand Rapids, Michigan 49530*

Library of Congress Cataloging-in-Publication Data

Spangler, Ann.
Immanuel : praying the names of God through the christmas season / Ann Spangler.
p. cm.
Includes bibliographical references.
ISBN-10: 0-310-27614-4 (alk. paper)
ISBN-13: 978-0-310-27614-2 (alk. paper)
1. Advent – Prayer-books and devotions. 2. Christmas – Prayer-books and devotions. 3. God (Christianity) – Name – Prayer-books and devotions. 4. Jesus Christ – Name – Prayer-books and devotions. I. Title.
BV40.S63 2007
242'.33 – dc22

2007001532

This edition printed on acid-free paper.

Interior design by Michelle Espinoza

Printed in the United States of America

---

07 08 09 10 11 12 • 18 17 16 15 14 13 12 11 10 9 8 7 6 5 4 3 2 1

Contents

Acknowledgments

Immanuel is adapted from two books that I have previously written: *Praying the Names of God* and *Praying the Names of Jesus.* In both cases, I am indebted to several people who supported me in significant ways throughout the time I was writing. Associate publisher and executive editor Sandy VanderZicht has proved both patient and wise as she critiqued the manuscripts in their original form. Senior editor at large Verlyn Verbrugge did his best to make sure that this nonscholar, nontheologian presented the material in a way consistent with both solid scholarship and sound theology. In addition, he offered many helpful suggestions about how best to adapt the material in this book for the Christmas season. I also want to extend special thanks to Michelle Espinoza for her creative and careful work on the interior design of the book. It has made a vital difference. I am grateful also to Sue Brower and Sherry Guzzy for their efforts to let the world know about the first two books, and to Karwyn Bursma for her team and for their efforts to spread the word about this one.

My hope is that God will use this book both to enrich your preparation and to enliven your celebration of the feast of Christmas, helping you to experience his love in fresh ways.

Pronunciation Guide to Names

Aster Lampros Proinos	as-TAIR lam-PROS pro-i-NOS
Basileus Basileon	ba-si-LEUS ba-si-LE-own
Emmanouel	em-man-ou-AIL
Iesous Soter	yay-SOUS so-TAIR
Immanu-el	im-ma-nu-AIL
Pais	PICE
Kokab Habboqer Habbahir	KO-kab hab-bo-QER hab-ba-HEER
Kyrios	KU-ree-os
Melek	ME-lek
Yahweh	yah-WEH
Yeled	YEL-ed
Yeshua	ye-shu-AH

A Deeper Wonder

Many children experience Christmas as a time of wonder. The sounds, smells, and sights of the season add up to a kind of magic that marks their lives forever. But children have little idea of how much effort and energy grown-ups expend to keep the magic going. Even as adults, many of us are still trying to recapture what we once felt, often without success.

Remember what happened in the movie version of *The Wizard of Oz* when the little dog, Toto, pulled back the curtain and revealed that the great and powerful Wizard was nothing but a carnival performer, a balloonist from Omaha who had been blown off course and landed in Oz? At the end of the story, the man behind the curtain sheepishly admitted to the disappointed Dorothy and her friends: "No, I'm afraid it's true. There's no other Wizard but me." Aren't we a little like him, standing now behind our own Christmas curtain, trying hard to perpetuate the magic?

Despite my misgivings, Christmas is still a big event in our home. We celebrate in all the usual ways—with family and friends, with good food, over-the-top decorations, and gifts spread beneath the tree. But rich as it is, Christmas doesn't produce the kind of wonder I used to experience when I still believed in elves and Christmas legends. Still, whenever I have taken time away from my frantic pursuits in order to focus on Christmas as a spiritual celebration, I have found a deeper wonder by far.

Like me, many people are beginning to discover or to rediscover the gift of Advent, a four-week-long season leading up to the celebration of Christmas. For centuries Christians have observed it as a way of reminding themselves of their hope—that Jesus, who came to us as a child two thousand years ago, has promised to return, this time to decisively defeat the darkness that threatens our world.

You may know that "advent" means "coming" or "arrival." Observing Advent is a way of preparing spiritually for Christmas so that our celebration produces a sense of joy and hope rather than feelings of cynicism and exhaustion. Advent, then, enables us to celebrate Christmas authentically. But do you know that Christmas itself was never meant to be merely a one-day event? Traditional celebrations of Christmas extend for a full twelve days.

So, four weeks for Advent and nearly two weeks for Christmas add up to six weeks—which is why I've put together six weeks of devotions, drawn from my books *Praying the Names of God* and *Praying the Names of Jesus,* to help you prepare. I want to give you something meaty to chew on as you consider the true and deep meaning of Christmas.

But why focus on the names and titles of Jesus in this season? Because in the ancient world names were thought to express a person's essential nature, character, or destiny. This is particularly true when it comes to the names of God revealed in the Scriptures. By knowing the names and titles of Jesus—ones like *Immanuel, King of Kings,* and *Bright Morning Star*—we come to know him better. We begin to perceive how deeply God loves us and how outrageous his plan to save us truly is.

Think about it—God fathered a child with a human being. And this child was born like any other—covered in blood, screaming for air, and attached to his mother by a fleshy cord. Together, God and a young woman produced a human being unique in the history of the world.

Even more amazing, this all-powerful, all-holy God allowed Mary and Joseph to take custody of his child. Arms that God himself had made would cradle divinity. The plan and purpose of God were accomplished through weakness, through human limitation, through dependency—through an infant who was as vulnerable to harm as anyone has ever been.

This, indeed, is scandal. It overthrows everything we ever thought about God. No longer is he a God who looks down on us from unreachable heights, disapproving us, measuring us, and finding us wanting. Instead, he is a tender Father, who cannot bear to be separated from his children, who, in fact, is driven to reveal the extent of his love by performing the greatest miracle of all—allowing his Son to become one of us, to take us by the hand and lead us out of darkness. This is a miracle we cannot fathom no matter how often we celebrate it.

I pray this year that your celebration of the feast of Christmas will be filled with peace and hope and with the firm assurance that no matter what you face in this world, you can still rejoice because God is near. Even now, one heart at a time, he is piercing the darkness with his steady, unquenchable light.

How to Use This Book

Immanuel is divided into six weeks. Each week is devoted to studying and praying a particular name of God. Here is how each week unfolds.

- The name page includes the English name of God and Jesus. Above it is the Hebrew equivalent and below it is the Greek equivalent.
- The next few pages contain a brief overview of the name as well as key Scripture passages that contain or pertain to the name.
- The Monday section is devoted to reading and studying. It provides a Scripture passage that reveals the name, background information, and a brief Bible study to help you understand the name.

- The Tuesday, Wednesday, and Thursday readings contain devotions to help you pray specific Scripture passages that contain the name or relate closely to it. The devotional readings are meant as a springboard for your own prayer! It will help to keep your Bible handy while reflecting on the relevant Scripture passages.
- The Friday reading will help you reflect on how the name connects to God's promises in Scripture. It offers key Bible promises that can be read, reflected on, or even memorized. A section "For Continued Prayer and Praise" lists additional passages related to the name that can be prayed on the weekend.

יהוה

Lord

κύριος

The Name

The Hebrew name *Yahweh* (yah-WEH) occurs more than 6,800 times in the Old Testament. It appears in every book but Esther, Ecclesiastes, and the Song of Songs. *Yahweh,* translated "LORD" in many Bibles, is the name that is most closely linked to God's redeeming acts in the history of his chosen people. We know who God is because of how he has acted on behalf of his people. When you pray to *Yahweh* this Christmas season, remember that he is the same God who draws near to save you from sin's tyranny just as he saved his people from their bondage in Egypt.

The Greek word *Kyrios,* translated "Lord" in the New Testament, could also at times be translated as "Yahweh." As you bow your head this week in prayer before Jesus, who is the sovereign Lord, remember that you are placing your life—the worst of your disappointments, the most protracted of your struggles, the wildest of your dreams—squarely in his hands. Knowing Jesus as Lord will lead you to a deeper experience of his presence and his power.

Key Scriptures

God said to Moses, "I AM WHO I AM. This is what you are to say to the Israelites: 'I AM has sent me to you.' "

God also said to Moses, "Say to the Israelites, 'The LORD [Yahweh], the God of your fathers—the God of Abraham, the God of Isaac and the God of Jacob—has sent me to you.' This is my name forever, the name by which I am to be remembered from generation to generation." *Exodus 3:14-15*

Therefore God exalted him to the highest place
    and gave him the name that is above every name,
that at the name of Jesus every knee should bow,
    in heaven and on earth and under the earth,
and every tongue confess that Jesus Christ is Lord,
    to the glory of God the Father.

Philippians 2:9-11

Monday

God Reveals His Name

The Scripture Reading

Now Moses was tending the flock of Jethro his father-in-law, the priest of Midian, and he led the flock to the far side of the desert and came to Horeb, the mountain of God. There the angel of the Lord appeared to him in flames of fire from within a bush. Moses saw that though the bush was on fire it did not burn up. So Moses thought, "I will go over and see this strange sight—why the bush does not burn up."

When the Lord saw that he had gone over to look, God called to him from within the bush, "Moses! Moses!"...

Moses hid his face, because he was afraid to look at God.

The Lord said, "I have indeed seen the misery of my people in Egypt. I have heard them crying out because of their slave drivers, and I am concerned about their suffering. So I have come down to rescue them....

"I am sending you to Pharaoh to bring my people the Israelites out of Egypt."

But Moses said to God, "Who am I that I should go to Pharaoh and bring the Israelites out of Egypt?"

And God said, "I will be with you. And this will be the sign to you that it is I who have sent you: When you have brought the people out of Egypt, you will worship God on this mountain."

Moses said to God, "Suppose I go to the Israelites and say to them, 'The God of your fathers has sent me to you,' and they ask me, 'What is his name?' Then what shall I tell them?"

God said to Moses, "I AM WHO I AM. This is what you are to say to the Israelites: 'I AM has sent me to you.'"...

"The elders of Israel will listen to you. Then you and the elders are to go to the king of Egypt and say to him, 'The LORD, the God of the Hebrews, has met with us. Let us take a three-day journey into the desert to offer sacrifices to the LORD our God.' But I know that the king of Egypt will not let you go unless a mighty hand compels him. So I will stretch out my hand and strike the Egyptians with all the wonders that I will perform among them. After that, he will let you go."

Exodus 3:1–4, 6–8, 10–14, 18–20

Today in the town of David a Savior has been born to you; he is Christ the Lord. *Luke 2:11*

Your attitude should be the same as that of Christ Jesus:

Who, being in very nature God,
did not consider equality with God something to be grasped,
but made himself nothing,
taking the very nature of a servant,
being made in human likeness.
And being found in appearance as a man,
he humbled himself
and became obedient to death—even death on a cross!
Therefore God exalted him to the highest place
and gave him the name that is above every name,
that at the name of Jesus every knee should bow,
in heaven and on earth and under the earth,
and every tongue confess that Jesus Christ is Lord,
to the glory of God the Father.

Philippians 2:5 - 11

Prayer

Lord, you are the same, yesterday, today, and forever—a God who listens to the cries of his people and who delivers us from our enemies. Thank you not only for delivering your people from bondage in Egypt but for delivering your people today from the deepest of all bondages—from our slavery to sin and death. We *know you now not only as our mighty God but as our humble Lord, the One who became like us so that we could become like you.*

Understanding the Name

As the sacred, personal name of Israel's God, the Hebrew name *Yahweh* was eventually spoken aloud only by priests worshiping in the Jerusalem temple. After the destruction of the temple in A.D. 70, the name was not pronounced at all. Instead, *Adonay* was substituted for *Yahweh* whenever it appeared in the biblical text. Because of this, the correct pronunciation of this name was eventually lost, and older translations of the Bible incorrectly translated the name as *Jehovah*. Modern English editions of the Bible usually translate *Adonay* as "Lord" and *Yahweh* as "LORD."

Unfortunately, the translation "LORD," which is a title rather than a name, obscures the personal nature of this name for God. Though the meaning of *Yahweh* is disputed, the mysterious self-description in Exodus 3:14, "I AM WHO I AM," may convey the sense not only that God is self-existent but that he is always present with his people. *Yahweh* is not a God who is remote or aloof but One who is always near, intervening in history on behalf of his people. The knowledge of God's proper name implies a covenant relationship. God's covenant name is closely associated with his saving acts in Exodus. The name *Yahweh* evokes images of God's saving power in the lives of his people.

Christianity's earliest confession of faith consisted of three short but incredibly powerful words: "Jesus is Lord!" The Greek word *Kyrios* (KU-ree-os) is used in the New Testament to refer to an owner, emperor, king, father, husband, or master. In addition to translating the Hebrew name *Yahweh,* it can also translate two Hebrew titles of God: *Adonay* and *Elohim.*

When people addressed Jesus as *Kyrios* or "Lord" in the Gospels, they were often simply showing respect to him as a rabbi or teacher, addressing him as "sir" rather than acknowledging him as God. But after his death and resurrection, the title "Lord" began to be widely used by believers.

Remember the apostle Thomas, who at first doubted accounts of Christ's resurrection? When Jesus appeared to him after his death, Thomas instinctively responded with a confession of faith: "My Lord and my God!" (John 20:28). Over time, the title *Kyrios* began to take on the characteristics of a name. As such, it clearly identified Jesus with *Yahweh,* the covenant name of God in the Hebrew Scriptures. Of the 717 passages in which *Kyrios* occurs in the New Testament, the majority are found in Luke's Gospel, the Acts of the Apostles, and Paul's writings.

Reflecting on the Name

Look at Exodus 3:1–20

- What does this passage reveal about what was in the heart of God in regard to his people?
- Moses' reluctance is not hard to understand. Describe a time when you were similarly reluctant to do something you thought God was calling you to do.
- Why do you think Moses asked God to reveal his name?

Look at Philippians 2:5–11

- How does God's idea of greatness differ from the usual definition?
- How have you experienced Jesus being Lord in your life?

Tuesday

Praying the Name

And God said, "I will be with you. And this will be the sign to you that it is I who have sent you: When you have brought the people out of Egypt, you will worship God on this mountain." ...

God said to Moses, "I AM WHO I AM. This is what you are to say to the Israelites: 'I AM has sent me to you.' "

God also said to Moses, "Say to the Israelites, 'The LORD [Yahweh], the God of your fathers – the God of Abraham, the God of Isaac and the God of Jacob – has sent me to you.' This is my name forever, the name by which I am to be remembered from generation to generation." *Exodus 3:12 - 15*

I am the LORD [Yahweh] your God, who brought you out of Egypt, out of the land of slavery. You shall have no other gods before me. *Exodus 20:2 - 3*

Reflect On: Exodus 3:12–15 and 20:2.
Praise God: For revealing himself through powerful acts of deliverance.
Offer Thanks: That God has freed you from every form of bondage.
Confess: Any tendency to forget what God has done for you.
Ask God: To help you remember his saving acts in your life.

"I AM WHO I AM." What do these mysterious words mean? Was Moses as bewildered as we are by God's self-disclosure? Or did he realize that God was assuring him he would always be present to his people—listening for their cries, answering their prayers, showing his power on their behalf, responding faithfully even when they acted faithlessly?

Yahweh. The name couldn't have clarified things. It may have sounded odd at first, like a name you warm to over time, much as an infant warms to the word "Mama," gradually equating her with safety, food, and help.

To the Egyptians the name Yahweh would have been a terror—a name to forget because it conjured plagues, darkness, defeat, and death. But to Moses and the Israelites Yahweh would forever mean deliverance, freedom, promise, and power. God's people could not invoke his name without remembering what it was like to walk through the parted waters of the Red Sea, to gather manna in the desert, to receive the commandments on Sinai.

The amazing events of Exodus defined who Yahweh was in extraordinary detail. Yahweh—Israel's faithful, wonder-working God, the One who out of pity and love reached into human history to untie the bonds of an enslaved people—that was the name by which this God wanted to be forever known.

Today in this Advent season, when you bow before Yahweh, thank him for the deliverance he has wrought in your own life through the work of Jesus. Acknowledge your continuing need for him and then recommit yourself to living by the Ten Commandments he gave, the law that enabled his people to live in his presence, confident of his care.

Wednesday

Praying the Name

An angel of the Lord appeared to him in a dream and said, "Joseph son of David, do not be afraid to take Mary home as your wife, because what is conceived in her is from the Holy Spirit. She will give birth to a son, and you are to give him the name Jesus, because he will save his people from their sins." *Matthew 1:20–21*

Jesus replied [to Jews who accused him of being demon-possessed], "If I glorify myself, my glory means nothing. My Father, whom you claim as your God, is the one who glorifies me. Though you do not know him, I know him. If I said I did not, I would be a liar like you, but I do know him and keep his word. Your father Abraham rejoiced at the thought of seeing my day; he saw it and was glad."

"You are not yet fifty years old," the Jews said to him, "and you have seen Abraham!"

"I tell you the truth," Jesus answered, "before Abraham was born, I am!" At this, they picked up stones to stone him, but Jesus hid himself, slipping away from the temple grounds. *John 8:54–59*

Reflect On: Matthew 1:20–21 and John 8:54–59.
Praise God: For foreseeing your need for a Savior.
Offer Thanks: For his delivering power.
Confess: Your continuing need for God's forgiveness.
Ask God: For a living understanding of what Jesus has done for you.

Christmas means lighted trees, presents, parties, and pageants full of pint-size shepherds and pudgy-faced angels proclaiming the birth of the Lord. We crane our necks, hoping our children won't botch their lines, smiling as they charmingly reenact the old story. We're full of Christmas cheer, happy to celebrate again with friends and family. It's a wonderful season. But in all our Christmas frenzy, we often forget to wonder—

- about what it was like for a poor man to find shelter for his pregnant wife.
- about the sound of the woman's cries as she gave birth in a dirty stable.
- about the audacity of God entrusting his own Son to two people who seemed hardly able to care for themselves.

Most of us also fail to wonder about the infant's name, given by an angel, a name linked to the holiest name in all of Scripture. For "Jesus" or Yeshua, a form of "Joshua," means this: "Yahweh is salvation." This time Yahweh was present with his people not in the form of a burning bush but in the shape of a small child who would later provoke people to violence precisely because he echoed God's self-revelation to Moses in the desert: "I tell you the truth, before Abraham was born, I am!"

Though Christmas Day may still be a few weeks away, this is a perfect day to bow down before our faithful, covenant-keeping God, praising him for the gift of his only Son, Jesus, the One who reminds us still that "Yahweh saves."

Thursday

PRAYING THE NAME

For you were once darkness, but now you are light in the Lord. Live as children of light (for the fruit of the light consists in all goodness, righteousness and truth) and find out what pleases the Lord.

Ephesians 5:8 - 10

Reflect On: Ephesians 5:8 – 10.
Praise God: Who gives us the grace to follow his Son.
Offer Thanks: For the ways in which the Lord has already reshaped your life.
Confess: Any tendency to resist the Lord.
Ask God: To make you eager to experience Jesus as Lord.

The apostle Paul uses the characteristic phrase "in the Lord" many times in his letters. He speaks about:

Believing in the Lord
Loving in the Lord
Working hard in the Lord
Boasting in the Lord
Being faithful in the Lord
Being strong in the Lord

Hoping in the Lord
Standing firm in the Lord
Rejoicing in the Lord

Paul even talks about being a *prisoner* in the Lord, and the book of Revelation makes it clear that it is possible to *die* in the Lord. Clearly, the early Christians considered Jesus to be not just their Savior but also their Lord. He was the atmosphere in which they lived, worked, prayed, suffered, and loved. They understood that their happiness depended not on having things their way, but on being completely aligned with Christ, uniting themselves to his character and purposes, regardless of the personal cost. And when Paul spoke about being "in the Lord," he was necessarily implying that it is possible to do things "outside of the Lord."

A friend of mine specializes in renovating old houses. When bidding on a job, Bill always begins by noting any structural defects or problems he discovers in the house. I was startled the first time I heard him refer to such defects as "sins." But the more I thought about it, the more sense it made because unless such problems are fixed, the house can never be restored to pristine condition. Likewise, sin has created an enormous structural problem in the world God made, allowing evil to deform it by threading its way through individuals, families, neighborhoods, institutions, and nations. To say that creation is off-kilter is to be guilty of an understatement.

But Jesus came to remedy this problem and to restore fallen creation, freeing it from enslavement to sin. His mission as Lord is to lead us out of captivity, to break sin's power, and he does this by saving us and then taking our disordered lives and reshaping them into his likeness. But how much like him we become depends on our giving constant consent to his lordship.

That's how we learn to do things "in the Lord." We know from Scripture that Christ will continue this work until the end of the world, when every kind of disorder—from petty squabbles to world wars, from thunderstorms to tsunamis, from diabetes to death (the ultimate disorder)—will cease to exist because everything and everyone will be exactly as God intends.

It is vital, then, that we know Jesus not only as Savior but also as Lord because that is the only way we can participate in building up his kingdom. Resisting his lordship, then, is more than a personal tragedy because it not only impedes the way God wants to work *in* us but also the way in which he wants to work *through* us. Our failures to believe and obey can have grave consequences for others.

Take a few moments today in this Advent season to be still in the Lord's presence. Bow your head before him, acclaiming him as *Kyrios*, your Lord forever. Then imagine your life in perfect alignment with his and let this picture become your prayer. Pray that Jesus will be all in all, working out his plans and extending his kingdom both in you and through you, world without end. Amen.

Friday

Promises Associated with His Name

What do you have in common with Billy Graham, Osama bin Laden, Stevie Wonder, and Sandra Day O'Connor? I can think of only one thing—each of you will someday bow your head and bend your knee with billions of others in the presence of the Lord. In his hands, all greatness, power, wisdom, and authority will be consolidated. Nothing of his power will remain hidden. Nothing will be held back. And you will see in his eyes either complete acceptance or complete rejection.

Now we see dimly. Then we will see clearly. Let us pray in this time of mercy for those who do not yet perceive Jesus as Lord. And let us pray for ourselves so that we are as ready as we can be for the great day of his coming.

Promises in Scripture

The LORD will be your confidence and will keep your foot from being snared. *Proverbs 3:26*

The name of the LORD is a strong tower; the righteous run to it and are safe. *Proverbs 18:10*

But do not forget this one thing, dear friends: With the Lord a day is like a thousand years, and a thousand years are like a day. The Lord is not slow in keeping his *promise, as some understand slowness. He is patient with you, not wanting anyone to perish, but everyone to come to repentance.*

But the day of the Lord will come like a thief. The heavens will disappear with a roar; the elements will be destroyed by fire, and the earth and everything in it will be laid bare. 2 Peter 3:8-10

You, then, why do you judge your brother or sister? Or why do you look down on your brother or sister? For we will all stand before God's judgment seat. It is written:

" 'As surely as I live,' says the Lord,
'every knee will bow before me;
every tongue will confess to God.' "

So then, we will all give an account of ourselves to God.
Romans 14:10-12

Continued Prayer and Praise

Meditate on God's self-description. (Exodus 34:4–7)

Pray this benediction, which includes the threefold repetition of Yahweh ("Lord"). (Numbers 6:24–27)

Remember that Yahweh is close to the brokenhearted. (Psalm 34:18)

Follow the Lord. (Mark 10:42–45)

Rejoice in the Lord. (Luke 2:8–14; Philippians 4:4)

Believe in the Lord. (John 20:24–29)

יֵשׁוּעַ

Jesus the Savior

Ἰησοῦς σωτήρ

The Name

Just as Yahweh is God's personal name revealed in the Old Testament, Jesus is the personal name of the One we call Redeemer, Lord, and Christ. His name is intimately linked to the God of the Hebrew Scriptures because the name Yeshua means "Yahweh is salvation."

Indeed, Jesus is Yahweh come to earth. If you have ever pictured God as a distant, wrathful Being, you will have to reconsider that portrait in light of Jesus Christ, who is God bending toward us, God becoming one of us, God reaching out in mercy, God humbling himself, God nailed to a cross, God rising up from the grave to show us the way home. Jesus, name above all names, beautiful Savior, glorious Lord!

Key Scripture

Praise be to the Lord, to God our Savior,
who daily bears our burdens. *Psalm 68:19*

Joseph son of David, do not be afraid to take Mary home as your wife, because what is conceived in her is from the Holy Spirit. She will give birth to a son, and you are to give him the name Jesus, because he will save his people from their sins. *Matthew 1:20–21*

Monday

God Reveals His Name

The Scripture Reading

This is how the birth of Jesus Christ came about: His mother Mary was pledged to be married to Joseph, but before they came together, she was found to be with child through the Holy Spirit. Because Joseph her husband was a righteous man and did not want to expose her to public disgrace, he had in mind to divorce her quietly.

But after he had considered this, an angel of the Lord appeared to him in a dream and said, "Joseph son of David, do not be afraid to take Mary home as your wife, because what is conceived in her is from the Holy Spirit. She will give birth to a son, and you are to give him the name Jesus, because he will save his people from their sins."

All this took place to fulfill what the Lord had said through the prophet: "The virgin will be with child and will give birth to a son, and they will call him Immanuel"—which means, "God with us."

When Joseph woke up, he did what the angel of the Lord had commanded him and took Mary home as his *wife. But he had no union with her until she gave birth to a son. And he gave him the name Jesus.*

Matthew 1:18-25

Prayer

Yeshua, my Savior. You are God forever and yet you became a little child. Thank you for saving me from all my sins. You reached down from on high to rescue me. Help me to live with the continual awareness of my need for your saving grace, now and always. Amen.

Understanding the Name

Luke's Gospel tells us that the infant Christ was given the name "Jesus" at the time of his circumcision, a name given him by the angel Gabriel, who appeared to his mother Mary (Luke 1:31; 2:21).

"Jesus" was a common name in first-century Palestine, and it has been found on various grave markers and tombs in and around Jerusalem. The full name of Barabbas, the insurrectionist Pilate released instead of Jesus, was probably Jesus Barabbas. To distinguish Jesus from others of the same name, he is sometimes referred to in the Gospels as Jesus of Nazareth, Jesus the son of Joseph, or Jesus the Nazarene. Later on, particularly in Acts and the New Testament letters, he is referred to as "Jesus Christ," as though Christ is his surname. By the second century the name "Jesus" had become so closely associated with Jesus of Nazareth that it nearly disappeared as a name given to either Christians or Jews.

The name "Jesus" (in English) or *Iesous* (in Greek) is the equivalent of the Hebrew *Yeshua* (ye-shu-AH), itself a contraction of the Hebrew name *Yehoshua*, translated "Joshua" in English Bibles. The name Joshua is the oldest name containing *Yahweh*, the Israelite covenant name of God, a name so sacred it was considered too holy to pronounce. Both "Jesus" and "Joshua" mean "Yahweh is help" or "Yahweh is salvation." *Yeshua* is also related to the word *yeshu'ah*, which means "salvation."

Soter is the Greek word translated "Savior." Its Hebrew equivalent is *Moshia*. In Greek, "Jesus the Savior" is rendered *Iesous Soter* (yay-SOUS so-TAIR). Through the centuries, the church has affirmed the belief of the earliest followers of Jesus that "salvation is found in no one else, for there is no other name given under heaven by which we must be saved" (Acts 4:12).

Reflecting on the Name

- What comes to mind when you hear the name "Jesus"?
- Though Jesus was a common name in first-century Palestine, God sent an angel to announce the name to Joseph. Comment on the significance of this.
- Why do you think Jesus' name is linked to the name of Yahweh, the covenant name of God in the Hebrew Scriptures?
- Describe what salvation means to you.

Tuesday

Praying the Name

Now the tax collectors and "sinners" were all gathering around to hear him. But the Pharisees and the teachers of the law muttered, "This man welcomes sinners and eats with them."

Then Jesus told them this parable: "Suppose one of you has a hundred sheep and loses one of them. Does he not leave the ninety-nine in the open country and go after the lost sheep until he finds it? And when he finds it, he joyfully puts it on his shoulders and goes home. Then he calls his friends and neighbors together and says, 'Rejoice with me; I have found my lost sheep.' I tell you that in the same way there will be more rejoicing in heaven over one sinner who repents than over ninety-nine righteous persons who do not need to repent."

Luke 15:1 – 7

But Zacchaeus stood up and said to the Lord, "Look, Lord! Here and now I give half of my possessions to the poor, and if I have cheated anybody out of anything, I will pay back four times the amount."

Jesus said to him, "Today salvation has come to this house, because this man, too, is a son of Abraham. For the Son of Man came to seek and to save what was lost."

Luke 19:8 – 10

Reflect On: Luke 15:1–7 and 19:8–9.
Praise God: Who is the Seeker of the lost.
Offer Thanks: Because God has pursued you.
Confess: Any complacency toward those who are lost.
Ask God: To align your heart with his purposes.

Rick Warren's *The Purpose Driven Life* stunned the publishing world by selling twenty-three million copies in just three years. The book's subtitle, "What on Earth Am I Here For?" poses a question most of us ask ourselves at least once a lifetime. But the most purpose-driven person in history may not have needed to pose the question at all because his purpose was announced before his birth.

Presumably Joseph, Mary's anxious husband-to-be, knew that *Yeshua* meant "Yahweh is salvation," but the angel in his dream was careful to spell it out for him: "You are to give him [the baby in Mary's womb] the name [*Yeshua*], because he will save his people from their sins" (Matthew 1:21). From the beginning the single purpose of Jesus' life was to seek out sinners and then to save them. He was God hunting souls, not to hurt them but to help them—and that is still his purpose.

I wonder how many of us really believe this. Do we have the slightest idea of how driven Christ is to dwell with the least attractive among us, with people who not only look bad but are bad? And if he has this drive to dwell with the worst and the lowest, doesn't that say something about his commitment to being with us when we are at our worst?

Theologian and writer Robert Farrar Capon has an interesting take on the parable Jesus told to disgruntled scribes and Pharisees about the shepherd who leaves ninety-nine *found* sheep in order to search for one *lost* sheep. The religious leaders had been grumbling about Jesus. How could a man with friends like tax collectors and sinners presume to teach them anything? It was against the backdrop of their self-righteousness that Jesus told them the parable, asking how they would respond if they owned a hundred sheep and one got lost.

Capon begins by pointing out that most shepherds wouldn't think of leaving ninety-nine sheep to go in search of one lost sheep because to do so would be to leave the rest of the flock vulnerable to predators. Instead, as Capon writes:

> You cut your losses, forget about the lost sheep, and go on with the ninety-nine.... In this parable, Jesus never goes back to the ninety-nine sheep. The ninety-nine sheep are a set-up. Jesus has divided the flock into one sheep and ninety-nine sheep.... I think the real meaning of the one and the ninety-nine is that the one lost sheep

is the whole human race as it really is. And the ninety nine "found" sheep who never get lost are the whole human race as we think we are.

No wonder Jesus liked to hang out around sinners. That's the only kind of people there are. As the parable implies, Jesus can do little for the strong and the self-righteous who don't even know they are lost. It's the poor, the weak, the addicted, the troubled, and the fractured people—those who have an inkling of how off course their lives have become who are often the most responsive to grace. This principle applies even after our conversion. Jesus seeks to bless the people who admit their need, not the ones who act as though they know it all and have it all. Blessed are the poor in spirit, the meek, those who hunger and thirst. Blessed are the empty, not the full.

Pray today, in this Christmas season, for the grace to know how much you still need Jesus. Ask him for the grace to see beyond your wants to the things you really need—more compassion and less harsh judgment, more generosity and less fear, more patience and less irritability, more faith and less doubt. Pray that Jesus will enable you to move beyond the kind of selfish praying we all do so that you can pray in a way that reflects his heart, letting whatever moves him move you. Then pray for the privilege of joining him as he seeks out and saves those who are lost.

Wednesday

Praying the Name

Once when we were going to the place of prayer, we were met by a slave girl who had a spirit by which she predicted the future. She earned a great deal of money for her owners by fortune-telling. This girl followed Paul and the rest of us, shouting, "These men are servants of the Most High God, who are telling you the way to be saved." She kept this up for many days. Finally Paul became so troubled that he turned around and said to the spirit, "In the name of Jesus Christ I command you to come out of her!" At that moment the spirit left her. *Acts 16:16 - 18*

Reflect On: Acts 16:16–18.
Praise God: For manifesting his power and authority through Jesus, his Son.
Offer Thanks: For the surpassing power of Jesus Christ.
Confess: Any occasions on which you have taken the Lord's name in vain.
Ask God: To lift up the name of his Son in your life.

There's power in the name of Jesus, even wonder-working power. But the name "Jesus" is not some kind of magical incantation. Invoking it is not like rubbing a lamp to conjure a genie. No, the power of the name of Jesus is released when people earnestly cry out to him and when they live in submission to him.

I've heard many stories that drive this home. One was told by a woman in my church. While walking to her car in a deserted garage one night, a thug accosted her, knife in hand. Though she was terrified, this woman managed to command her would-be mugger, carjacker, rapist, murderer, or whoever he was: "Get away from me in the name of Jesus!" To her astonishment, though they were alone in the garage, the man backed up as though someone had just threatened him with a knife. Then he turned and fled.

Then there's the story of E. P. Scott, a missionary to India. One day Scott decided to visit a mountain tribe who had never heard of Jesus. But as he approached the mountain, a band of angry tribesmen surrounded him with spears pointed straight at his chest. On impulse, the missionary took out the violin he was carrying, closed his eyes, and began playing and singing a hymn in their native language. When Scott finally found the courage to open his eyes, he was amazed to see that his attackers had dropped their spears and that several of them had tears in their eyes. Scott spent the rest of his life preaching and serving the people of that tribe, many of whom became believers. What was the hymn he sang? "All Praise the Power of Jesus' Name!"

Jim Cymbala, pastor of the Brooklyn Tabernacle, tells a more recent story about a homeless heroin addict named Danny Velasco. Though his friend Wanda had shared the gospel with him, Danny dismissed it as so much nonsense. After living on the street for three years he had contracted Hepatitis A, B, and C, and his 108-pound body was covered with sores. Passersby could hear him talking like a crazy man to the swarm of voices that screamed in his head. This is what happened when Danny landed in a hospital in the Bronx, seemingly on his deathbed:

> When I woke up, I found myself in a bed, covered in my own vomit. Suddenly all the voices in my head started screaming, creating total chaos within me. I was so disoriented, I wanted to die! But I couldn't jump out a window because they were barred.
>
> Then, in the midst of all my pain, something or someone whispered words I had heard before: *The day you call on the Lord, he will set you free.* All the other voices tried to drown it out, but they couldn't! I don't know if it was an angel or the Holy Spirit, but the words came through clearly: "The day you call on the Lord, he will set you

> free." In absolute desperation I screamed from my bed, "Jesus help me! O God, help me with everything! You're my only hope, so please help, Jesus!" I didn't understand anything about prayer, so I even used "personal references" as I cried out: "Jesus, Wanda said that when I called on your name, you would deliver me. So help me now, O God."
>
> At that moment Almighty God swept over me and around me. I knew he was real because all the voices in my head suddenly stopped their hellish screaming and the ball of fear that had been weighing on me lifted. I knew everything had changed even though nothing outwardly had—I was still lying in my vomit in a hospital bed in the Bronx. But I was a million miles from where I had been before I said that prayer.

Eleven years later, Danny is alive and well, a million miles from the hopeless addict he had been before he cried out to Jesus. The demons that plagued him could not withstand the power of the name of Jesus. His story affirms the words of another popular hymn, reminding us that "at the name of Jesus, every knee shall bow, every tongue confess him, King of glory now!"

Thursday

Praying the Name

[The angel said to the shepherds,] "Today in the town of David a Savior has been born to you; he is the Messiah, the Lord. This will be a sign to you: You will find a baby wrapped in cloths and lying in a manger."

Suddenly a great company of the heavenly host appeared with the angel, praising God and saying,

> "Glory to God in the highest heaven,
>   and on earth peace to those on whom his favor rests." *Luke 2:11 – 14*

With this in mind, we constantly pray for you, that our God may count you worthy of his calling, and that by his power he may fulfill every good purpose of yours and every act prompted by your faith. We pray this so that the name of our Lord Jesus may be glorified in you, and you in him, according to the grace of our God and the Lord Jesus Christ. *2 Thessalonians 1:11 – 12*

Reflect On:	Luke 2:11–14 and 2 Thessalonians 1:11–12.
Praise God:	For the greatness of his glory.
Offer Thanks:	Because God has created you to be his image bearer.
Confess:	Any tendency to be more concerned for your glory than for God's.
Ask God:	To fulfill his primary purpose for your life.

My daughters love things that sparkle—stars that glow in the dark, rainbow stickers, pink glittery wands. Through the years I have had to fend off many a request for gaudy red shoes "just like the ones Dorothy wore in Oz." I trace these attractions not so much to feminine stereotypes as to a basic human yearning. Boys display their own form of this yearning when they wear superhero capes and brandish plastic swords. But what is this yearning? It's a longing for something beautiful and shining and powerful, for something beyond ourselves that we can make a part of ourselves. It's a yearning for glory.

But what does this yearning have to do with Jesus as Savior? To begin with, it is important to realize that Jesus' saving work has both negative and positive dimensions. First, we are saved *from* something—Jesus rescues us from God's wrath directed at our sins. Second, we are saved *for* something—Jesus saves us so that we can fulfill the primary purpose for which God made us. Think for a moment of a time when you sat by the edge of the ocean or by a lake, transfixed by the beauty of the waves as sunlight danced across them. That's a picture of how we are meant to reflect God's glory to the world. We are to shine with his presence, power, and love.

Scripture is full of this notion. The book of Daniel tells of a time when those who belong to God "will shine like the brightness of the heavens ... like the stars for ever and ever" (Daniel 12:3). Paul assures the Roman Christians: "I consider that our present sufferings are not worth comparing with the glory that will be revealed in us" (Romans 8:18). Additional passages speak of "the Lord of glory," "Christ in you, the hope of glory," and "the crown of glory that will never fade away."

This craving for glory seems to be imbedded in our spiritual DNA. It is something God has hardwired into our souls. But sin has so distorted the human genome that our search for glory is often misguided. We look for it in flimsy, temporal things, such as success, money, relationships, personal charm, and beauty—none of which can ultimately satisfy. No matter how many sparkling red shoes we own or how many superhero capes we don, we find they are never enough.

Carol Cymbala, director of the Brooklyn Tabernacle Choir, gives us a glimpse of what it means to seek true glory.

> The Brooklyn Tabernacle Choir doesn't perform. We haven't provided backup to musical superstars or sung at national political conventions, even though we've been asked to more than once. Our call, our greatest joy, is to worship God, and to lead other Christians to experience him in worship. We also want to sing the message of the gospel to those who don't know Christ. So week after week, we open our hearts to him eagerly waiting, painfully aware that if God doesn't come to meet us, we will never accomplish our purpose.
>
> We are not naïve about the dangers that come with apparent success, because we know that self-aggrandizement displeases God. And God won't bless us if we're out to please ourselves. I tell the choir, "God has allowed us to win six Grammys. But there are better choirs out there. The only reason he's blessed us is so he can use us to reach more people. So just remember who you are, and I'll remember who I am. Apart from God we're nothing."

Carol means what she says. She understands that worldly glory is like tinsel compared to God's glory. In this Advent season as you worship *Yeshua*, the Lord of glory, give in to your appetite for glory by praying the refrain from Graham Kendrick's well-known song:

> Shine, Jesus, shine!
> Fill this land with the Father's glory.
> Blaze, Spirit, blaze!
> Set our hearts on fire.
> Flow, river, flow!
> Flood the nations with grace and mercy.
> Send forth your word,
> Lord, and let there be light.

Friday

Promises Associated with His Name

The hurricane that devastated New Orleans in the fall of 2005 left us with images we will never forget. Day after day, we saw people perched on rooftops, desperately waiting for someone to rescue them. Many of them must have wondered if their world was about to end. Everywhere they looked—death, destruction, danger. The scenes were pitiful, heartrending, frightening.

This is a powerful picture of what life would be like were it not for Jesus, who is himself the greatest of all the promises in the Bible. Even his name is a promise—*Yahweh is salvation.* He is rescue, help, deliverance. Remember this in your times of trial. Call on his name. Trust in his name. Live in his name. Let the name "Jesus" be the first prayer you pray in the morning and the last prayer you say at night. Jesus, the only name by which we can be saved.

Promises in Scripture

Peter replied, "Repent and be baptized, every one of you, in the name of Jesus Christ for the forgiveness of your sins. And you will receive the gift of the Holy Spirit. The promise is for you and your children and for *all who are far off—for all whom the Lord our God will call."* Acts 2:38-39

Jesus did many other miraculous signs in the presence of his disciples, which are not recorded in this book. But these are written that you may believe that Jesus is the Christ, the Son of God, and that by believing you may have life in his name. John 20:30-31

Continued Prayer and Praise

Believe in the power of Jesus' name. (Matthew 12:15–21; John 3:16; Acts 3:1–10; 4:1–12; Romans 5:9–11)

Rejoice when you are found worthy to suffer for the sake of the name. (Acts 5:40–42; 21:10–14)

Do everything in the name of the Lord Jesus. (Colossians 3:15–17)

Trust in Jesus for salvation. (Titus 3:3–8)

עִמָּנוּ אֵל

Immanuel

Ἐμμανουήλ

The Name

The name "Immanuel" appears twice in the Hebrew Scriptures and once in the New Testament. In Greek, it is rendered "*Emmanouel.*" One of the most comforting of all the names and titles of Jesus, it is literally translated "with us is God" or, as Matthew's Gospel puts it, "God with us." When our sins made it impossible for us to come to him, God took the outrageous step of coming to us, of making himself susceptible to sorrow, familiar with temptation, and vulnerable to sin's disruptive power, in order to cancel its claim. In Jesus we see how extreme God's love is. Remember this the next time you feel discouraged, abandoned, or too timid to undertake some new endeavor. For Jesus is still Immanuel—he is still "God with us."

Key Scriptures

Then Isaiah said, "Hear now, you house of David! Is it not enough to try the patience of human beings? Will you try the patience of my God also? Therefore the Lord himself will give you a sign: The virgin will conceive and give birth to a son, and will call him Immanuel."

Isaiah 7:13 - 14

All this took place to fulfill what the Lord had said through the prophet: "The virgin will conceive and give birth to a son, and they will call him Immanuel" (which means "God with us"). *Matthew 1:22 - 23*

Monday

God Reveals His Name

The Scripture Reading

This is how the birth of Jesus Christ came about: His mother Mary was pledged to be married to Joseph, but before they came together, she was found to be with child through the Holy Spirit. Because Joseph her husband was a righteous man and did not want to expose her to public disgrace, he had in mind to divorce her quietly.

But after he had considered this, an angel of the Lord appeared to him in a dream and said, "Joseph son of David, do not be afraid to take Mary home as your wife, because what is conceived in her is from the Holy Spirit. She will give birth to a son, and you are to give him the name Jesus, because he will save his people from their sins."

All this took place to fulfill what the Lord had said through the prophet: "The virgin will be with child and will give birth to a son, and they will call him Immanuel" – which means, "God with us."

Matthew 1:18 - 23

Prayer

Immanuel, I praise you for your faithful love – drawing near when I was far from you. Instead of casting me away from your presence, you came to call me home. Instead of punishing me for my sins, you came to free me from them. Immanuel, my God, you are here with me today. Live in me and glorify your name, I pray.

Understanding the Name

The name "Immanuel" (im-ma-nu-AIL) first appears in Isaiah 7:14 as part of a prophetic word that Isaiah spoke to King Ahaz of Judah (the southern kingdom) at a time when Syria and Israel (the northern kingdom) had formed a coalition against Assyria, the region's greatest power. They wanted Judah to join their uprising. The prophet Isaiah counseled Ahaz to trust in the Lord rather than to appeal to Assyria for help against Syria and Israel, who were threatening to invade Judah for refusing to join them. Then he invited Ahaz to ask the Lord for a sign to confirm the prophetic word, but the unfaithful king refused, having already decided to place his trust not in the Lord but in Assyria.

In response to Ahaz's refusal to trust God, Isaiah proclaimed: "Hear now, you house of David! Is it not enough to try the patience of human beings? Will you try the patience of my God also? Therefore the Lord himself will give you a sign: The virgin will be with child and give birth to a son, and will call him Immanuel" (Isa. 7:13–14).

Shortly after that Syria and Israel were soundly defeated, exactly as Isaiah had prophesied. Many years later the southern kingdom of Judah was destroyed by Babylon, its people taken captive.

Matthew's Gospel recalls Isaiah's prophecy, applying it to the child who would be born of Mary, the virgin betrothed to Joseph. The sign given hundreds of years earlier to an apostate king was meant for all God's people. In fact the Bible is nothing if not the story of God's persistent desire to dwell with his people. In Jesus, God would succeed in a unique way, becoming a man in order to save the world not from the outside, but from the inside. *Immanuel, God with us*, to rescue, redeem, and restore our relationship with him.

Reflecting on the Name

- How have you experienced "Immanuel"—God being with you, in your life thus far?
- Matthew begins and ends his Gospel (see Matthew 28:20) with the promises that God is with us. How would your life be different if you began and ended each day with the firm belief that God is with you?
- What does this title of Jesus reveal about his nature?

Tuesday

PRAYING THE NAME

"Go away from me, Lord; I am a sinful man!"

Luke 5:8

Where can I go from your Spirit?
Where can I flee from your presence?
If I go up to the heavens, you are there;
if I make my bed in the depths, you are there.
If I rise on the wings of the dawn,
if I settle on the far side of the sea,
even there your hand will guide me,
your right hand will hold me fast.

Psalm 139:7-10

Reflect On: Psalm 139:7–10 and Luke 5:8.
Praise God: For his promise to be with you.
Offer Thanks: For God's persistence in pursuing you.
Confess: Any pattern of sin in your life.
Ask God: To increase your confidence in his desire to be with you.

One of the most profound of all the promises in the Bible is this: *I am with you*. Matthew implied it about Jesus in the Christmas story, and Jesus said it to his disciples (and to us) at the end of that same Gospel: "Surely I am with you always, to the very end of the age." If the Lord is with us, what do we have to fear? What do we lack? How can we lose? The same Lord who walked on water, healed the sick, and rose from the dead is saving us, watching over us, guiding our steps. Knowing this, why don't we dance in the streets and throw more parties? Why do we instead often act as though God is not only *not* with us but that he is nowhere in the vicinity?

There may be many reasons why we feel God's absence in our lives. One of these is surely that our "spiritual sensors" don't work very well. We are like malfunctioning radar that can't spot a supersonic jet flying straight overhead. But another common reason is that we are the ones who go AWOL, not God.

Consider Peter. One day Jesus climbed into Peter's boat, telling him to row out into the lake and cast his nets out despite the fact that Peter had been up all night fishing with nothing to show for it. But this time when Peter threw out the nets, he caught so many fish that his boat began to sink. Instead of jumping with joy, Peter fell down and implored Jesus to leave him, saying, "Go away from me, Lord; I am a sinful man!"

There's something right about Peter's response. Jesus is holy and sin is his implacable enemy. Still, the Lord didn't leave Peter. Instead he stayed and transformed his life. And that's what Jesus wants to do with our lives. We make a mistake when we let our sin drag us down and away from the One who has promised to be with us. Instead of running to him, we let a cloud settle over us. Finding it hard to pray, we move farther away. In a thousand different ways, we say, "Depart from me, O Lord!"

At times like this we need to recall the words of Psalm 139:11–12:

> If I say, "Surely the darkness will hide me
> and the light become night around me,"
> even the darkness will not be dark to you;
> the night will shine like the day,
> for darkness is as light to you.

If you are troubled by some persistent failing, by some entrenched sin, don't run away from Jesus. Instead express your sorrow and ask for his forgiveness—and then receive it. After that pray this famous fourth-century prayer known as St. Patrick's Breastplate:

> Christ be beside me, Christ be before me,
> Christ be behind me, King of my heart;
> Christ be within me, Christ be below me,
> Christ be above me, never to part.
>
> Christ on my right hand, Christ on my left hand,
> Christ all around me, shield in the strife;
> Christ in my sleeping, Christ in my sitting,
> Christ in my rising, light of my life.

Christ be beside me, Christ be before me,
Christ be behind me, King of my heart;
Christ be within me, Christ be below me,
Christ be above me, never to part.

Wednesday

Praying the Name

I am with you and will watch over you wherever you go, and I will bring you back to this land. I will not leave you until I have done what I have promised you.
Genesis 28:15

You have been a refuge for the poor,
a refuge for the needy in his distress,
a shelter from the storm
and a shade from the heat. *Isaiah 25:4*

Reflect On: Genesis 28:15 and Isaiah 25:4.
Praise God: Because he is present, even in the midst of great suffering.
Offer Thanks: For all the ways the Lord has watched over you.
Confess: Your inability to reflect Christ's presence without his grace.
Ask God: To open your eyes to the ways he is at work in the world and in your own life.

What if God had jurisdiction only in your city, county, or state? Leaving the area would mean leaving behind his protection and care, putting yourself outside the circle of his influence. At such times you wouldn't even bother praying to him because he could neither hear nor help you. Odd as it sounds, that's precisely how many ancient people thought about their gods. They believed in gods whose power was limited to a particular region or locality.

But listen to what God said to Jacob when he was on the run from Esau, the brother whose birthright he had stolen: "I will watch over you wherever you go." Clearly, this God was not confined to a particular territory or region. His protection and power were available wherever his people went. Indeed, as they were to discover, his power extends over the whole earth.

Many of us are taught this truth as little children, barely able to mouth the bulky words—God is omnipresent and omnipotent, everywhere and all-powerful. Yet as we grow older, some of us find ourselves restricting him, shrinking him down, setting boundaries around his ability and his love. I caught myself doing this a couple of years ago as I listened to media reports of a tropical storm that slammed into Haiti. More than 1,500 people drowned, and another 1,300 were missing, many of them swept out to sea or buried beneath debris. Of those who survived, many of the 300,000 homeless were perching on rooftops or living on debris-strewn sidewalks where the water had subsided.

But it got worse. Unburied bodies, raw sewage, and animal carcasses were everywhere, and there was not enough food to feed the living. Without adequate roads and supplies, relief efforts seemed like Band-Aids pasted over gaping wounds. How could anyone, I wondered, solve Haiti's intractable problems? It seemed like such a God-forsaken place.

As I prayed, I began to realize that God isn't the one who is absent in Haiti or in any other part of the world. It may only seem that way because so many of us are absent, withholding our prayers because of our little faith, withholding our gifts because of our little love. True, we can't do everything, but we can do something. We can tackle the problem that is in front of us, helping to bring God's presence to those who suffer.

If we want to experience Immanuel, "God with us," we need to be where he is, to do what his love compels, to reflect his image to the rest of the world. Today, I pray that Christ will pierce my heart with the things that pierce his. I ask for the grace to look for him in the midst of the world's suffering, whether close to home or far away. I pray that he will give you and me the faith to join him there, transforming our prayers, our time, our talents, and our financial resources into evidence of his presence in the world—Immanuel, a God who is truly with us, in this Christmas season and every day of the year.

Thursday

Praying the Name

As the Father has loved me, so have I loved you. Now remain in my love. If you obey my commands, you will remain in my love, just as I have obeyed my Father's commands and remain in his love. I have told you this so that my joy may be in you and that your joy may be complete. My command is this: Love each other as I have loved you. John 15:9–12

Don't you know that you yourselves are God's temple and that God's Spirit lives in you? 1 Corinthians 3:16

Reflect On: John 15:9–12 and 1 Corinthians 3:16.
Praise God: For calling you to be his image bearer.
Offer Thanks: That God lives in you.
Confess: Any failures that mar the image of God in you.
Ask God: To show you how to bear his image, to magnify him by expressing his love to others.

Randy Frame was part of a team of journalists and business leaders invited to Haiti in the mid-1990s to view its problems close up. Trained as a reporter to maintain his distance, Randy wasn't prepared for what happened on the last day of his trip.

That day the group visited *La Cay Espwa*, the "House of Hope," a refuge for starving children cared for by a small group of nuns. As soon as Randy entered the two-room structure, a nun by the name of Sister Conchita approached, offering him the child she cradled in her arms. Reluctant at first to take the child lest he violate his role as an objective observer, Randy finally gave in, deciding it would be rude to refuse.

"Her name Maria," the Sister said with broken English and a quiet smile.

Frame writes:

> I took Maria into my arms, gingerly at first. She seemed so fragile: I could practically see the skeleton beneath her skin. Only her eyes seemed to have escaped the circumstances of her young life. Her eyes were deep brown and as shiny as any healthy child's ought to be. She focused them not on me, but on Sister Conchita. It was clear I was "second string." Perhaps my arms were not as soft or comfortable. Yet she didn't cry. Maybe she was too weak to protest being held by a stranger. Or perhaps she was glad to be in anyone's arms. How could I tell?

After they left, Randy's tour guide explained that on average one in four of the children in the House of Hope dies because of the damage that chronic hunger wreaks on the body. You can spot the ones who won't make it. Lethargic, with pale, rigid skin, their hair has a reddish hue. The guide could have been describing Maria.

Despite being warned about the danger of venturing out alone in Port-au-Prince, Randy left the security of his hotel that night to make the two-mile trek back to the House of Hope. When he found Sister Conchita, she was still sitting on her rocker with Maria in her arms.

> As I approach Sister Conchita, she stands, sensing exactly why I have returned. She says nothing, but offers me the child. And also her chair.... I have arrived at the place where I want to be. And as I live out what I'd earlier in the day envisioned, I am suddenly and fully aware of my weaknesses, my limitations. And aware also of the limitations and shortcomings of humanity, which has somehow failed this child and many others like her....
>
> I am utterly powerless to determine whether this child, who bears the image of God, will live or die this night. But I do have power—complete power—to make certain that if and when her frail body finally yields, she has felt the security, the

comfort, of someone's loving arms. Tonight they are my arms. It's the least I can do for her, and also, perhaps, the most. Her weak but gracious eyes look up to mine. And hold their gaze. And in the sacred silence of this moment, there is no other power I crave, no other purpose I desire.

Randy's story made me sad—and happy. God's love is so evident. It is "God with us," "God with Randy," "God with Maria"—the Lord expressing himself to and through human beings. Like Randy, we are called to be Christ-bearers, to reflect God to others. Today let us ask for the grace to make Immanuel known, to allow his light and his life to shine through us.

Friday

Promises Associated with His Name

What does it mean to say that God is with us? Surely it doesn't mean our lives will be easy. It doesn't mean we will be insulated from failure or doubt or that God will take our side in every argument. But it does mean we will never face even a single struggle alone. It means the Lord will never withhold the help we need to do his will. It means that ultimately we will come out on top even if we feel we're living most of our life on the bottom.

What difficulties are you facing? Chronic illness? Troubled children? A broken marriage? Financial hardship? Take a moment today to stop imagining yourself surrounded by all your difficulties and instead begin to envision yourself as you really are—surrounded by the presence of your faithful God. Invoke his name—Immanuel. Decide today to do everything in your power to follow him. Then ask for his peace, pray for his protection, and open your life to his power.

Promises in Scripture

But Moses said to God, "Who am I, that I should go to Pharaoh and bring the Israelites out of Egypt?"

And God said, "I will be with you." *Exodus 3:11-12*

I will never leave you nor forsake you. . . . Have I not commanded you? Be strong and courageous. Do not be terrified; do not be discouraged, for the LORD your God will be with you wherever you go. *Joshua 1:5, 9*

When you pass through the waters,
  I will be with you;
and when you pass through the rivers,
  they will not sweep over you.
When you walk through the fire,
  you will not be burned;
  the flames will not set you ablaze.
For I am the LORD, your God,
  the Holy One of Israel, your Savior.
Isaiah 43:2–3

Surely I am with you always, to the very end of the age. *Matthew 28:20*

Keep your lives free from the love of money and be content with what you have, because God has said,

"Never will I leave you;
  never will I forsake you."

So we say with confidence,

"The Lord is my helper; I will not be afraid.
  What can human beings do to me?"
Hebrews 13:5–6

Continued Prayer and Praise

Pray this verse when you are afraid. (Joshua 1:9)

Be encouraged because no one can prevail against you if God is with you. (Isaiah 8:10)

Remember that Jesus will not leave us orphans. He will show himself to those who love him. (John 14:15–21)

יֶלֶד

Child

παῖς

The Name

A child was always at the heart of the biblical covenant. Already in the garden of Eden God promised that Eve's offspring would crush the head of the serpent, who beguiled her. Later God made a covenant with Abraham, promising that Sarah would bear him a child who would be the first of countless descendents. Then Isaiah spoke of a child who would be born of a virgin and be given the name "Wonderful Counselor, Mighty God, Everlasting Father, Prince of Peace." The New Testament tells of the fulfillment of that promise in the Christmas stories, and Jesus presents children as the model for his followers to emulate. The only way to enter the kingdom is with the humility and trust of little children.

Key Scripture

For to us a child is born,
  to us a son is given. . . . *Isaiah 9:6*

Joseph also went up from the town of Nazareth in Galilee to Judea, to Bethlehem the town of David, because he belonged to the house and line of David. He went there to register with Mary, who was pledged to be married to him and was expecting a child. While they were there, the time came for the baby to be born, and she gave birth to her firstborn, a son. She wrapped him in cloths and placed him in a manger, because there was no room for them in the inn. *Luke 2:4–7*

Monday

God Reveals His Name

The Scripture Reading

In those days Caesar Augustus issued a decree that a census should be taken of the entire Roman world. (This was the first census that took place while Quirinius was governor of Syria.) And everyone went to his own town to register.

So Joseph also went up from the town of Nazareth in Galilee to Judea, to Bethlehem the town of David, because he belonged to the house and line of David. He went there to register with Mary, who was pledged to be married to him and was expecting a child. While they were there, the time came for the baby to be born, and she gave birth to her firstborn, a son. She wrapped him in cloths and placed him in a manger, because there was no room for them in the inn.

And there were shepherds living out in the fields nearby, keeping watch over their flocks at night. An angel of the Lord appeared to them, and the glory of the Lord shone around them, and they were terrified. But the angel said to them, "Do not be afraid. I bring you good news of great joy that will be for all the people. Today in the town of David a Savior has been born to *you; he is Christ the Lord. This will be a sign to you: You will find a baby wrapped in cloths and lying in a manger." Luke 2:1 - 12*

Prayer

Lord, you were cradled in human arms and laid in a manger. How can I begin to understand a gift so unexpected? That someone so great would allow himself to become so small? Help me to follow you, like a little child, laying aside my pretensions and admitting my need. Help me to love you, trust you, and lean on you today, and thank you for showing me the way into your kingdom.

Understanding the Name

Though the Israelites considered children a great blessing, they occupied the bottom rung of the social ladder. Entrusted with the solemn responsibility of teaching and disciplining them, parents were accorded nearly absolute authority over their children. To be a child was to be powerless, dependent, subservient. Yet even little children and young infants could receive wisdom from God and their lips could praise him. The prophet Isaiah spoke of a child, or *yeled* (YEL-ed), who would one day be born of a virgin and sit on David's throne. Luke's Gospel tells us that Mary, while she was yet betrothed, was expecting a child, or *pais* (PICE), and that she gave birth to him in Bethlehem.

Reflecting on the Name

- What images come to mind when you think of the child Jesus?
- Why do you think Luke mentions that Jesus was born in Bethlehem and that he was Mary's son?
- Why do you think God allowed his Son to be born in such humble circumstances and to be placed in a manger?

Tuesday

Praying the Name

For to us a child is born, to us a son is given.

Isaiah 9:6

In a loud voice she [Elizabeth] exclaimed: "Blessed are you among women, and blessed is the child you will bear!" *Luke 1:42*

Reflect On: Isaiah 9:6 and Luke 1:26–45.
Praise God: For keeping his promise to his people.
Offer Thanks: That God's ways are so much higher than ours.
Confess: Your tendency to rely more on yourself than you do on God.
Ask God: For the grace to depend on him like children depend on their father and mother.

One of the reasons I find the gospel so convincing is that it's nothing I would have dreamed up. Think about what God did. He became a human baby, who like any other infant had to be fed, burped, and bathed. He allowed himself to get the flu, to be teased, to stub his toe like any other little kid. To be thought the illegitimate son of a teenage mother. To have for his main defense against an irate king a human father without an ounce of political pull. And that's just the beginning.

What if I had been God? Would I have devised an all-loving strategy to woo my people back to myself, developing a plan that would require weakness, humility, and dependency on the part of my child? I doubt it. My strategy would probably have involved more power than love because power seems less risky.

From a distance of two thousand years, it can be difficult to comprehend how shocking the incarnation was and still is. It's true that the Jewish people had been awaiting a child who would become Israel's deliverer, ushering in a golden age in which God's people would finally come out on top. No more oppression. No more bondage. Little wonder that every woman wanted to be that child's mother. But even in her wildest dreams, no Jewish woman would have thought that would have meant cradling God in her arms. God's gracious plan was beyond anything his people could have imagined.

The apostle Paul speaks of Christ's crucifixion as "the foolishness of God." But surely God's foolishness began when he allowed his Son to be born in a stable and laid in a manger. In fact, the life of Jesus was nothing but divine foolishness at work, trumping human wisdom and exposing it as folly.

Jesus puts it to his disciples like this: "Unless you change and become like little children, you will never enter the kingdom of heaven. Therefore, whoever humbles himself like this child is the greatest in the kingdom of heaven" (Matthew 18:3–4). Like everything else he demanded of his disciples, Jesus lived the pattern before he asked it of them. But what does it mean to become like little children?

Most children don't have much money. They don't have a lot of power. They often lack wisdom. And they aren't afraid to ask for help. Hasn't Jesus already made it plain? If you want to be big in God's kingdom, become small in this world. If you want to save your life, be willing to lose it.

During the Advent season, God is calling you to become like a little child, asking you to follow him with humility and trust. Decide to embrace his "foolish-seeming" plan for your life, confident that his strength will be perfected through your weakness. Guard against self-reliance and self-promotion. Try to find ways to humble yourself, committing yourself to following Christ in childlike trust and obedience.

Wednesday

Praying the Name

When they [the Magi] had gone, an angel of the Lord appeared to Joseph in a dream. "Get up," he said, "take the child and his mother and escape to Egypt. Stay there until I tell you, for Herod is going to search for the child to kill him."

So he got up, took the child and his mother during the night and left for Egypt, where he stayed until the death of Herod. And so was fulfilled what the Lord had said through the prophet: "Out of Egypt I called my son."

When Herod realized that he had been outwitted by the Magi, he was furious, and he gave orders to kill all the boys in Bethlehem and its vicinity who were two years old and under. *Matthew 2:13-16*

Reflect On: Matthew 2:13–20.
Praise God: For never abandoning his plan to save us.
Offer Thanks: Because even as a child, Jesus shared our suffering.
Confess: Any tendency to hide your faith for fear of opposition.
Ask God: To increase your understanding of the gospel.

Christmas—it's not about a baby! That was the surprising message of a talk I listened to a few years back. I don't remember everything the speaker said, but I am certain he must have opened one too many Christmas cards depicting the Christ child as a cherubic babe, surrounded by velvety soft animals more suited to the pages of a children's book than a stable. He didn't want the celebration of the great feast of the incarnation to be reduced to something sentimental and saccharine. In fact, the Lord's birthday story is a dramatic and richly layered narrative that bears careful rereading. You could say it contains the DNA of the gospel, linking the child Jesus to Israel's past as well as to its future. It is like a seed that encapsulates the unfolding story of salvation—past, present, and to come.

For instance, Matthew's Gospel begins with a long genealogy linking Jesus to Abraham, Isaac, Jacob, David, and Solomon. Then, after recounting Jesus' birth and the visit of the Magi, the story shifts because already opposition to the Christ child is rising. An angel appears to Joseph in a dream, warning him that Herod is searching everywhere for Jesus, intending to murder him. So Joseph flees with Jesus and Mary to Egypt. Like Moses, the child Jesus is rescued only in the nick of time. Enraged that the Magi have left without telling him the precise location of the newborn king, Herod orders all the boys of Bethlehem two years old and under to be slaughtered, echoing Pharaoh's decree that every Hebrew male infant be drowned in the Nile River.

It's the Exodus story in miniature. From the very beginning, Jesus is linked to the suffering history of his people, to their exile and oppression. His life recalls the words of Hosea: "When Israel was a child, I loved him, and out of Egypt I called my son" (Hosea 11:1).

The nativity story links Jesus not only to his people's past but also to their future. To shepherds tending their flocks outside Bethlehem, an angel proclaims: "I bring you news of great joy that will be for all the people. Today in the town of David a Savior has been born to you; he is Christ the Lord. This will be a sign to you: You will find a baby wrapped in cloths and lying in a manger" (Luke 2:10–12). The shepherds were amazed, telling everyone about him. They had seen their long-awaited Savior, the desire of all nations, the One who would one day refer to himself as the Good Shepherd.

So Christmas, the great feast of the incarnation, *is* about a baby after all. And *it's not* about a baby. It's about the great story of God's love as it stretched across the centuries toward its climax in the life of the child Jesus. No wonder Simeon held the boy in his arms when his parents brought him to the temple, speaking these words to Mary: "This child is destined to cause the falling and rising of many in Israel, and to be a sign that will be spoken against, so that the thoughts of many hearts will be revealed" (Luke 2:34–35).

Even as a child, Jesus created turbulence in the world. His mere existence demanded a response. Either love him or hate him, accept his message or try to quash it. Why then should we be surprised when we encounter opposition because of our faith? If we bear the image of Christ within us, we will certainly cause offense to some. But many others will welcome the Jesus they see in us. Pray today that Christ will shine more brightly in your heart and in every heart that belongs to him because God wants to reveal his Son to a world that is dying to know him.

Thursday

Praying the Name

So Joseph also went up from the town of Nazareth in Galilee to Judea, to Bethlehem the town of David, because he belonged to the house and line of David. He went there to register with Mary, who was pledged to be married to him and was expecting a child. While they were there, the time came for the baby to be born, and she gave birth to her firstborn, a son. She wrapped him in cloths and placed him in a manger, because there was no room for them in the inn. *Luke 2:4–7*

Reflect On: Luke 2:1–20.
Praise God: For speaking to us through his Son.
Offer Thanks: For all the ways God has provided for you and your family, materially and spiritually.
Confess: Any failure to value God's Word enough to read it regularly.
Ask God: To nourish you through his Word.

Remember the lyrics to the Christmas hymn "Silent Night"?

Silent night! holy night!
All is calm, all is bright

Round yon virgin mother and child,
Holy infant, so tender and mild –
Sleep in heavenly peace,
Sleep in heavenly peace.

A story is told of a first grader who drew a picture of the nativity for his Sunday school class. After complimenting him on his artistic ability, his teacher inquired about the round figure lurking in the corner of his drawing. Surprised that she hadn't recognized him, the boy responded, "Oh, that's round John Virgin!"

At a distance of two thousand years, it can be easy to get some of the details wrong. How many of us, for instance, picture Mary riding a donkey into Bethlehem? But the Bible never tells us whether Mary walked or rode on an animal. The only donkeys in the story are the ones that populate our crèche sets. And what about the three Magi who worshiped the infant in the stable? The Bible never specifies how many Magi were there, though it does say they presented Jesus with three gifts. But at least we know they worshiped the infant in the stable, right? Sorry! Matthew's Gospel says Jesus was living in a house by the time the Magi arrived in Bethlehem. Some biblical scholars think he may have been a two-year-old by the time they caught up with him.

While none of these details significantly alters the meaning of the story, we sometimes miss details that do.

Take the manger, for instance. There's no disputing the fact that the Bible says Mary placed her baby in a feeding trough shortly after his birth. This detail highlights the humble circumstances surrounding his birth. We know that. But how many of us have ever wondered if there's more to it—another reason why God's Son began his life in a feeding trough? Could God have been telegraphing a message, hoping we would understand that Jesus would become a source of nourishment for his people, feeding and sustaining us throughout our lives?

As you read Scripture today remember that Jesus wants to nourish you—to share his life with you. Take time to meditate on what you are reading, asking his Spirit to give you understanding. As you meditate on God's Word, remember that meditation simply means to ponder or to *chew on* something. Instead of going away hungry, ask God today to help you feed on his Word, to let it satisfy your longings and fill up your empty places.

Friday

Promises Associated with His Name

I was forty-six when I adopted my first child—not as old as the biblical Sarah but a far sight older than Mary, the teenage mother of Jesus. But no matter how old you are or how long you've waited, a child can be one of life's greatest blessings, opening you again to wonder, renewing your amazement at God's good plan for the future.

Little wonder that a child was God's first promise to the world. After Adam and Eve sinned, as they were being forced from their garden paradise, God made the most hopeful of all his promises, assuring them that Eve's offspring would one day crush the serpent whose temptation had pushed them out of Eden and into so much misery. No wonder Mary has sometimes been called the new Eve, her obedience a striking reversal of Eve's disobedience. And as for the Christ child—he has always been identified as the fulfillment of God's promise to crush Satan, our worst enemy, and as the one who would lead us back to paradise.

Promises in Scripture

So the Lord *God said to the serpent, "Because you have done this,*

"*Cursed are you above all the livestock*
and all the wild animals!
You will crawl on your belly
and you will eat dust
all the days of your life.
And I will put enmity
between you and the woman,
and between your offspring and hers;
he will crush your head,
and you will strike his heel." Genesis 3:14 - 15

Therefore the Lord himself will give you a sign: The virgin will be with child and will give birth to a son, and will call him Immanuel. Isaiah 7:14

Continued Prayer and Praise

Praise God for promising a child who would reign forever with his justice and righteousness. (Isaiah 9:6–7)

Strive to be the greatest in the kingdom of heaven. (Matthew 18:2–4; Luke 9:48)

מֶלֶךְ

King; King of Kings

βασιλεὺς βασιλέων

The Name

The Israelites believed that Yahweh was *Melek,* or King—not just over Israel but over every nation on earth. They understood that the temple in Jerusalem was the earthly symbol of God's heavenly throne, and they expected a coming Messiah who would one day save his people from their enemies, establishing his rule over the whole world.

The New Testament presents Jesus as the King of kings, whose perfect obedience ushered in the kingdom of heaven. Though he entered the world humbly, as an infant born in Bethlehem, Magi from the east still recognized him as the newborn king. And though his reign unfolds in hidden ways, he has promised to come again, at which time he will reveal himself unambiguously as "King of kings and Lord of lords." When you pray to Jesus, the King of kings, call to mind his mastery not only over human beings but over nature, disease, and death itself.

Key Scripture

For the LORD *is the great God,*
the great King above all gods. *Psalm 95:3*

On his robe and on his thigh he has this name written:

KING OF KINGS AND LORD OF LORDS.

Revelation 19:16

Monday

God Reveals His Name

The Scripture Reading

Endow the king with your justice, O God,
the royal son with your righteousness.
He will judge your people in righteousness,
your afflicted ones with justice.
The mountains will bring prosperity to the people,
the hills the fruit of righteousness.
He will defend the afflicted among the people
and save the children of the needy;
he will crush the oppressor.
He will endure as long as the sun,
as long as the moon, through all generations.
He will be like rain falling on a mown field,
like showers watering the earth.
In his days the righteous will flourish;
prosperity will abound till the moon is no more.
He will rule from sea to sea
and from the River to the ends of the earth....
All kings will bow down to him
and all nations will serve him.

For he will deliver the needy who cry out,
  the afflicted who have no one to help.
He will take pity on the weak and the needy
  and save the needy from death.
He will rescue them from oppression and violence,
  for precious is their blood in his sight.
Long may he live! *Psalm 72:1-8, 11-15a*

As they approached Jerusalem and came to Bethphage on the Mount of Olives, Jesus sent two disciples, saying to them, "Go to the village ahead of you, and at once you will find a donkey tied there, with her colt by her. Untie them and bring them to me. If anyone says anything to you, tell him that the Lord needs them, and he will send them right away."

This took place to fulfill what was spoken through the prophet:

"Say to the Daughter of Zion,
  'See, your king comes to you,
gentle and riding on a donkey,
  on a colt, the foal of a donkey.' "

Matthew 21:1-5

I saw heaven standing open and there before me was a white horse, whose rider is called Faithful and True. With justice he judges and makes war. His eyes *are like blazing fire, and on his head are many crowns. He has a name written on him that no one knows but he himself. He is dressed in a robe dipped in blood, and his name is the Word of God. The armies of heaven were following him, riding on white horses and dressed in fine linen, white and clean. Out of his mouth comes a sharp sword with which to strike down the nations. "He will rule them with an iron scepter." He treads the winepress of the fury of the wrath of God Almighty. On his robe and on his thigh he has this name written:*

KING OF KINGS AND LORD OF LORDS.

Revelation 19:11 - 16

Prayer

Lord, help me in this Advent season to seek first your kingdom, forsaking my desire to build my own small kingdom. Give me the grace to actively await your coming by loving my enemies, doing good to those who hate me, serving the poor, and spreading the good news of your kingdom wherever I go.

Understanding the Name

Compared to surrounding nations, the Israelites were relatively late in adopting monarchy as a form of government. Instead, they thought of Yahweh as their King. Once the monarchy was established, it was understood that the king received his power from God and was therefore responsible for ruling according to God's laws. David, Israel's second king, for the most part represented the ideal of how a king should rule. But most of the kings of Israel and Judah fell far short of the ideal, leading people away from God by forging ill-fated alliances with foreign powers and by sanctioning the worship of false gods.

Because the Jewish people longed for a king who would be descended from David, it is hardly surprising that the crowd who greeted Jesus as he entered Jerusalem hailed him as the "Son of David." They expected their messianic king to restore Israel's freedom and former glory. In the passage from Matthew's Gospel, Jesus fulfills the messianic prophecy of Zechariah 9:9 by riding into Jerusalem on a donkey, an animal that symbolized both peace and humility.

The passage from Revelation 19, which speaks of a time when Christ's kingly rule will be fully established, presents Jesus riding not on a lowly donkey but on a magnificent white horse, as befits the greatest of all kings. Throughout the New Testament Jesus is variously referred to as "King," "King of the ages," "King of the Jews," "King of Israel," and "King of kings"—this last one translated from the Greek phrase *Basileus Basileon* (ba-si-LEUS ba-si-LE-own). Even today some Christian churches are called "basilicas," a phrase meaning "the hall of the king."

Reflecting on the Name

Look at Psalm 72

- This psalm may have been a coronation prayer for one of the Davidic kings. Though it doesn't directly refer to God as the King, it does reflect the values of our heavenly King. Describe these.

Look at Matthew 21:1–9 and Revelation 19:11–16

- Why do you think Scripture presents the reign of Jesus in two such different ways, as in the above passages?
- Write a list of qualities that would describe the perfect king. Now compare and contrast these with the lives of today's rulers.
- What do you think it means to have Jesus as your king? How have you experienced his reign in your life thus far?
- What would life on earth look like today if Jesus' reign was perfectly established?

Tuesday

Praying the Name

A shoot will come up from the stump of Jesse;
    from his roots a Branch will bear fruit.
The Spirit of the Lord will rest on him—
    the Spirit of wisdom and of understanding,
    the Spirit of counsel and of power,
    the Spirit of knowledge and of the fear of the
    Lord....
Righteousness will be his belt
    and faithfulness the sash around his waist.
The wolf will live with the lamb,
    the leopard will lie down with the goat,
the calf and the lion and the yearling together;
    and a little child will lead them....
The infant will play near the hole of the cobra,
    and the young child put his hand into the
    viper's nest.
They will neither harm nor destroy
    on all my holy mountain,
for the earth will be full of the knowledge of the
    Lord
    as the waters cover the sea.

Isaiah 11:1-2, 5-6, 8-9

Reflect On:	Isaiah 11:1–9.
Praise God:	For he is the true King.
Offer Thanks:	For the ways God has already used you to build up his kingdom.
Confess:	Any tendency to live as though this world is all there is.
Ask God:	To fill the earth with the knowledge of him.

Several years ago I nearly met a king. I was touring Israel and Jordan with a small group of editors and writers interested in learning more about the intractable problems of the region. During our time in Amman, Jordan, our tour director attempted to arrange a meeting with His Majesty King Hussein bin Talal, known to his people as *Al-Malik Al-Insan*, "The Humane King." But the king was busy that day. So we met, instead, with his younger brother, His Royal Highness Prince El Hassan bin Talal, who was then the crown prince. Afterward, we crowded around on the steps of the palace to have our photograph taken with him, commemorating our one brief brush with royalty.

Like most Americans, I find the idea of royalty exotic, romantic, and rather antiquated. And no wonder. Monarchs and monarchies have suffered a long decline throughout the world. If you doubt it, try an Internet word search for "king." You are more likely to turn up "Burger King,"

"B. B. King," "Martin Luther King," "Stephen King," *The Lion King*, or even "Elvis Presley" than the name of a reigning monarch.

But the Bible pictures God as the greatest Monarch of all. Far from being in decline, God's rule extends over the entire universe. Though challenged by the one Jesus called "the prince of this world," God still reigns.

Isaiah presents a shocking though beautiful image of what the world will be like when God's rule is perfectly and permanently established: "The infant will play near the hole of the cobra"; "the wolf will live with the lamb"; "the leopard will lie down with the goat"; and "a little child will lead them." The world in perfect harmony. No violence, no hatred, no hurt. Nothing out of sync, out of control, off kilter. The weak and the strong living happily together, world without end. Evil will vanish, becoming merely an archaic word in the celestial dictionary.

Next time you read the newspaper or watch the nightly news, contrast Isaiah's vision of the world as it will one day be with your vision of the world as it currently is. Pray for the grace to perceive more deeply and to participate more fully in the work God is doing to build up his kingdom right now. Remember the words of Jesus shortly before his death: "Those who love their life will lose it, while those who hate their life in this world will keep it for eternal life. Whoever serves me must follow me; and where I am, my servant also will be" (John 12:25–26). Then join your prayer to his:

> *Our Father in heaven,*
> *hallowed be your name*
> *your kingdom come,*
> *your will be done*
> *on earth as it is in heaven.* Matthew 6:9-10

Wednesday

Praying the Name

God is the King of all the earth. *Psalm 47:7*

Jesus told them another parable: "The kingdom of heaven is like a man who sowed good seed in his field. But while everyone was sleeping, his enemy came and sowed weeds among the wheat, and went away. When the wheat sprouted and formed heads, then the weeds also appeared.

"The owner's servants came to him and said, 'Sir, didn't you sow good seed in your field? Where then did the weeds come from?'

" 'An enemy did this,' he replied.

"The servants asked him, 'Do you want us to go and pull them up?'

" 'No,' he answered, 'because while you are pulling the weeds, you may root up the wheat with them. Let both grow together until the harvest. At that time I will tell the harvesters: First collect the weeds and tie them in bundles to be burned; then gather the wheat and bring it into my barn.' " *Matthew 13:24–30*

Reflect On:	Psalm 47 and Matthew 13:24–30.
Praise God:	The King of the whole earth.
Offer Thanks:	For God's patience.
Confess:	Any complacency you may have regarding the return of the King.
Ask God:	To hasten the coming of his Son.

If God is King of the whole world, why is the world such a mess? Couldn't an all-powerful God do something about the poverty, crime, and suffering that have been part of the world's story from the beginning? Wouldn't an all-loving God want to?

The question nags. It's hard to ignore. It demands our attention. Perhaps it will help if we consider two things: First, there's opposition. Satan (the word means "Adversary") is a spiritual being, a fallen angel, who opposed God's rule and in so doing ushered sin into the world. And sin is at the root of every misery the world has ever suffered.

Second, though God could have instantly destroyed Satan and sinners (that's all of us), he decided to take the long way round, quelling the world's rebellion not by brute force but by the power of divine love. That strategy requires restraint. It takes patience. It means justice in a final sense has to be delayed. It means evil is played out to the bitter end so that love can draw as many people as possible into the kingdom. To say it another way, the weeds and the wheat are allowed to grow up together until the world's last day.

On that day Jesus will no longer hide himself but will step boldly into history, not veiling his power but appearing in all his brilliance as King of kings and Lord of lords, judging the world with his justice and establishing his reign on the earth.

As we wait for the King's return (remember that "advent" means "coming"), let's spread the kingdom by sharing the good news, feeding the hungry, serving the poor, and loosening the bonds of the oppressed. Also, let us allow the values of the kingdom to shine forth in us by the way we think and act and pray. Then, anticipating that final day of the Lord, let us bow down and worship, proclaiming Jesus as our King and Lord forever.

Thursday

Praying the Name

Our Father in heaven,
hallowed be your name,
your kingdom come,
your will be done
on earth as it is in heaven. *Matthew 6:9-10*

Then he said to his disciples, "The time is coming when you will long to see one of the days of the Son of Man, but you will not see it. People will tell you, 'There he is!' or 'Here he is!' Do not go running off after them. For the Son of Man in his day will be like the lightning, which flashes and lights up the sky from one end to the other. But first he must suffer many things and be rejected by this generation. *Luke 17:22-25*

Reflect On: Matthew 6:9–10 and Luke 17:22–25.
Praise God: Because he is a perfect Ruler.
Offer Thanks: That Christ has promised to come again.
Confess: Any complacency in your relationship with Christ.
Ask God: To stir up your longing for his coming again in glory.

King Farouk of Egypt once wryly predicted the end of his reign, remarking that "in a few years there will be only five kings in the world—the king of England and the four kings in a pack of cards." But Farouk, the last real king of Egypt, was leaving out the greatest King of all.

Last year as Christmas approached, I wanted to avoid making the same mistake. But what does Christmas have to do with acknowledging Jesus as King? In many churches throughout the world, Advent is observed as a season in which we prepare spiritually to celebrate Christ's first coming. It is also a season to prepare our hearts for his second coming, when every knee will bend and every tongue will confess that he indeed is King and Lord.

I wanted to find a way to make Advent a central part of our family's celebration of Christmas. To do this, I had to make some practical decisions. A few years ago, I was surprised to learn that my grandparents never trimmed their Christmas tree until the night before Christmas. Apparently, it was a common practice back then. So, for me that was the first order of business—to resist the urge to decorate and shop and party as though Christmas arrived the day after Thanksgiving. No more nonstop Christmas music. No more franticness. I decided to let the season's meaning unfold in calmness.

Despite the protests of my children who saw everyone else's decorations going up, I was determined that Advent would not become an endangered species in our house. I did allow them one concession, but it played perfectly into my Advent scheme. I made the traditional candy house, the delectable one my mother had made for me as a child, placing it as always in a prominent spot in the living room. And as always I reminded them of rule number one: no eating—not one bite—until Christmas morning. There were the usual murmured complaints, but I knew my children were learning the Advent discipline of waiting with eager expectation.

For my part, I made no superhuman efforts to observe the season, but simply made sure I finished most of my Christmas shopping before Thanksgiving. Then I prayed a little more. In the morning and evening I read Scriptures that expressed a longing for the Messiah, for peace on earth, for captives to be set free, for the lion and lamb to lie down together. I read about the Bright Morning Star and the Light of the World. And I read the news—the kidnappings, the beheadings, the battles, the political wrangling, and the poisoning of a political opponent. I read about the man in a wheelchair who had frozen to death in my city because of people's carelessness—and I interceded with anguish for Christ to set things right, to bring justice and peace, forgiveness and mercy. I prayed with longing and tears that he would come with his power and his wisdom to reign over us.

As Christmas draws near this year, I find that I am glad for the baby born in Bethlehem, but that I am longing for the greatest of kings. I see how broken the world is, how broken I am, without him. As I have prayed in the weeks leading up to Christmas, I find my thoughts returning to the day in which the World Trade Center towers collapsed. I remember sitting in a hospital room with my daughter, who was about to undergo a medical test. We sat transfixed in front of the TV, watching as New York came under attack—planes crashing, people jumping out of buildings, the city devastated. We watched the Pentagon burning. It seemed surreal, so sudden and impossible—the financial heart and the power center of the greatest country on earth both under attack. Like everyone else who watched, it changed our perception of the world.

Since then, I have not found it difficult to believe in Christ's sudden coming. In an instant, in a flash, in the twinkling of an eye, at the last trumpet—the dead will be raised imperishable and we will all be changed, and the greatest of all kings will ascend his throne.

Maranatha! Come, Lord Jesus!

Friday

Promises Associated with His Name

Jesus promised his followers that they would inherit the kingdom of God, prepared for them since the beginning of time. Take a few moments to consider what your life would look like if you really believed that in just a few short years, you were going to inherit a kingdom, filled with everything your heart desired. This would be a place so marvelous that in it you would never be lonely, confused, or bored. A place so peaceful that you would always love and be loved, understand and be understood. Every need, every desire would be perfectly fulfilled.

Wouldn't this knowledge put things in an entirely different perspective? Would life be nearly as frantic? Would you expend so much energy stockpiling the goods of this world? Or would you find a new ease settling into your soul and a growing desire to get ready for the world to come by reflecting its values right here and right now?

Promises in Scripture

The LORD will be king over the whole earth. On that day there will be one LORD, and his name the only name. *Zechariah 14:9*

The righteous will shine like the sun in the kingdom of their Father. *Matthew 13:43*

Then the King will say to those on his right, "Come, you who are blessed by my Father; take your inheritance, the kingdom prepared for you since the creation of the world." *Matthew 25:34*

Then I saw a new heaven and a new earth, for the first heaven and the first earth had passed away, and there was no longer any sea. I saw the Holy City, the new Jerusalem, coming down out of heaven from God, prepared as a bride beautifully dressed for her husband. And I heard a loud voice from the throne saying, "Now the dwelling of God is with men, and he will live with them. They will be his people, and God himself will be with them and be their God. He will wipe every tear from their eyes. There will be no more death or mourning or crying or pain, for the old order of things has passed away." *Revelation 21:1-4*

Continued Prayer and Praise

Pray for the increase of God's government. (Isaiah 9:6–7)

Worship the King of glory. (Psalm 24)

Prepare for the King's return. (Matthew 24:9–14; Luke 19:11–26; 1 Timothy 6:11–16; 2 Peter 1:5–11)

Approach the throne of grace with confidence. (Hebrews 4:16)

Envision the throne of God and of the Lamb. (Revelation 22:1–5)

כּוֹכַב הַבֹּקֶר הַבָּהִיר

Bright Morning Star

ἀστὴρ λαμπρὸς πρωϊνός

The Name

In the last chapter of the book of Revelation, Jesus calls himself the "bright Morning Star." In ancient times, the morning star was thought of as a herald of the new day, signaling the dawn of hope and joy. The brightest object in the sky aside from the sun and moon, it is a fitting type for Christ, who ushers in a new day for the entire world. When you call on Jesus, the Bright Morning Star, you are calling on the One from whom all darkness flees.

Key Scriptures

> The oracle of one who hears the words of God,
> who has knowledge from the Most High,
> who sees a vision from the Almighty,
> who falls prostrate, and whose eyes are opened:
> "I see him, but not now;
> I behold him, but not near.
> A star will come out of Jacob;
> a scepter will rise out of Israel."
>
> *Numbers 24:16 – 17*

I am the Root and the Offspring of David, and the bright Morning Star. *Revelation 22:16*

Monday

God Reveals His Name

The Scripture Reading

I see him, but not now;
  I behold him, but not near;
A star will come out of Jacob;
  a scepter will rise out of Israel.

Numbers 24:17

Behold, I am coming soon! My reward is with me, and I will give to everyone according to what he has done. I am the Alpha and the Omega, the First and the Last, the Beginning and the End.

Blessed are those who wash their robes, that they may have the right to the tree of life and may go through the gates into the city. Outside are the dogs, those who practice magic arts, the sexually immoral, the murderers, the idolaters and everyone who loves and practices falsehood.

I, Jesus, have sent my angel to give you this testimony for the churches. I am the Root and the Offspring of David, and the bright Morning Star.

Revelation 22:12 – 16

Prayer

Lord, you are the brightest of all stars. I pray that you will chase away the world's darkness and the shadows that linger in my life. Help me to await your coming with hope and confidence and to long eagerly for the new day that will never end, the day in which your kingdom will be finally and fully established.

Understanding the Name

What the Bible refers to as the morning star is actually the planet Venus, known since prehistoric times. As the second planet from the sun, it is also one of the hottest. A relatively young planet, it is Earth's closest neighbor and is often called our sister planet. Because of its appearance in the eastern sky before dawn, it was thought of as the harbinger of sunrise. The title *Aster Lampros Proinos* (as-TAIR lam-PROS pro-i-NOS) presents a powerful and beautiful image of the One who is also known as "the light of the world."

Though this title does not appear in the Hebrew Scriptures, the book of Numbers refers to a coming star, a scepter that will rise up out of Israel. *Kokab Habboqer Habbahir (*KO-kab ha-bo-QER ha-ba-HEER) is Hebrew for "Bright Star of the Morning."

Reflecting on the Name

- Jesus says that he is coming soon. In what ways do you think his second coming will differ from his first?

- Describe your attitude toward the second coming—fear, doubt, hope, joy? Why do you feel the way you do?
- What kinds of people is Jesus describing in the passage from Revelation?

Tuesday

Praying the Name

After Jesus was born in Bethlehem in Judea, during the time of King Herod, Magi from the east came to Jerusalem and asked, "Where is the one who has been born king of the Jews? We saw his star in the east and have come to worship him." *Matthew 2:1-2*

I, Jesus, have sent my angel to give you this testimony for the churches. I am the Root and the Offspring of David, and the bright Morning Star. *Revelation 22:16*

Reflect On: Matthew 2:1–12 and Revelation 22:16.
Praise God: For shining his light into our world.
Offer Thanks: For the ways God has shed his light on you.
Confess: Any hidden sins, which fester in the darkness.
Ask God: To make you eager for the new life he gives you.

"Light therapy" is the treatment of choice for a depressive condition called Seasonal Affective Disorder, commonly known as SAD. Though the diagnosis may sound trendy, anyone who lives in a climate that gets only a little winter sunlight is not likely to doubt it. Many of us would be the first to patronize a restaurant like the one in Helsinki, Finland, that from October to March serves bright light with breakfast. Every morning the Café Engel places light boxes throughout the restaurant so that, along with a Danish and coffee, patrons can get their fix of light.

It seems obvious that our bodies are wired for light. Without enough of it, some of us are prone to weight gain, irritability, anxiety, sleeplessness, and stress. But it's not only our bodies that suffer in the darkness. Our souls long for the light as well. Perhaps that's why the story of Jesus is associated with light from start to finish.

Remember the brilliant star that led the Magi from the east to the child Jesus in Bethlehem? Some scholars think the "star" was the light produced by the conjunction of Jupiter and Saturn, which happened three times in 7 BC. Such a celestial event would have been of particular interest at that time because Jupiter was commonly associated with kingly rule and Saturn with the Jewish people. To the Magi, the star of Bethlehem was a sign that a glorious kingdom was about to dawn.

So, the life of Jesus begins with a "star," and you can say that it also ends with a star, because in the last chapter of the Bible the risen Lord calls himself the "bright Morning Star," a reference to the planet Venus, the brightest object in the predawn sky except for the moon — the sure sign that dawn will soon break over the world.

Two thousand years later, we can echo the words of the Magi concerning the newborn king: "We saw his star when it rose and have come to worship him" (Matthew 2:2). Because of Jesus, a new day, bright with promise, has dawned on the entire world. Or, to put it another way, Jesus is the most powerful light therapy ever invented. He is the One who destroys our darkness by the light of his presence.

This week, try imprinting this name on your heart by choosing a day to rise early. As you watch the sun come up, you may even spot Venus rising in the east. In those predawn moments, praise the risen Christ, the Bright Morning Star, who has come to shine his light on you.

Wednesday

Praying the Name

I see him, but not now;
    I behold him, but not near.
A star will come out of Jacob;
    a scepter will rise out of Israel. *Numbers 24:17*

He [Jesus] replied, "When evening comes, you say, 'It will be fair weather, for the sky is red,' and in the morning, 'Today it will be stormy, for the sky is red and overcast.' You know how to interpret the appearance of the sky, but you cannot interpret the signs of the times." *Matthew 16:2-3*

Reflect On: Numbers 24:17 and Matthew 16:2–3.
Praise God: For giving us signs of his presence.
Offer Thanks: For all the ways God has guided you.
Confess: Any confusion that comes from taking your eyes off Jesus.
Ask God: To help you stay the course by fixing your eyes on him.

Have you ever wondered how ancient mariners were able to navigate without using a compass? One trick was to watch the flight paths of birds. Norse sailors knew that a seabird with a full beak was heading to its rookery on land while a bird with an empty beak was probably heading out to sea in search of food.

The Phoenicians, like many seafaring peoples that followed, were sophisticated enough to rely on the sky to get them through the treacherous seas. By watching the sun in its path, they knew whether they were heading east or west. They could also locate their position by gazing at the night sky, aware as they were that individual stars appear at fixed distances above the horizon at any particular location and time of year. Even today, satellites use a similar technique, marking their position in space by using "star trackers," instruments that use groups of stars as reference points.

What does any of this have to do with Christ as the bright Morning Star? Remember that the morning star was considered the harbinger of dawn. When Jesus called himself the "bright Morning Star," he was saying that he is our reference point—the sign that a new day is dawning on the world. Scripture tells us that this will be a day that will never end. Its light will be so steady, strong, and fixed that darkness will finally be banished from the earth. No more sin, no more sorrow, no more tears. If the first coming of Jesus is like the star that announces the dawn, his second coming will be like lightning, bringing the swift fulfillment of his kingdom.

Like the ancient mariners, who were able to read the skies, we need to remember to look up, to lift our faces to the Bright Morning Star, because it is only when Jesus is our reference point that we understand our true location in space and time.

Jesus faulted the religious leaders of his day for failing to interpret the signs of the times. Let us pray today for the grace to be like wise seafarers, joyful when they saw the morning star rising in the east.

Thursday

Praying the Name

We did not follow cleverly invented stories when we told you about the power and coming of our Lord Jesus Christ, but we were eyewitnesses of his majesty. For he received honor and glory from God the Father when the voice came to him from the Majestic Glory, saying, "This is my Son, whom I love; with him I am well pleased." We ourselves heard this voice that came from heaven when we were with him on the sacred mountain.

And we have the word of the prophets made more certain, and you will do well to pay attention to it, as to a light shining in a dark place, until the day dawns and the morning star rises in your hearts. *2 Peter 1:16 - 19*

Reflect On: 2 Peter 1:16–19.
Praise God: For bringing you into the light of his presence.
Offer Thanks: Because God has a unique purpose for your life.
Confess: Any tendency to resist God's purpose because of fear or insecurity.
Ask God: To strengthen your hope.

I graduated from college during the midst of a recession. Armed with a combined degree in psychology, sociology, and political science, my résumé didn't place me at the top of any employer's wish list. For the first few months, the best job I could find was at a small spring and wire factory serving the auto industry. The work was so monotonous I thought I would lose my mind. And I wasn't the only one. Every night when the bell rang, workers stampeded to the exits to see who could be the first out. Worse yet, the day started before sunrise and ended after sundown. The daily commute in the darkness seemed like a metaphor for my life. In contrast to friends who had landed promising jobs in San Francisco, Los Angeles, Washington, DC, New York, and Dallas, I felt futureless. Stuck in the Midwest with a meaningless job, I couldn't have scripted a more depressing start to the rest of my life.

Back then I didn't realize my life was a story God was writing. As far as I knew, I had grabbed the pen right out of his hand, refusing to believe he even existed. I was intent on enjoying life on my terms, determined to write my life the way I wanted it to be. Trouble was, I seemed to be suffering from writer's block.

Looking back, I realize God hadn't entirely let go of the script. He was using the shadows—my insecurity and fears—to drive me toward his light. When I finally admitted the truth—that I was headed nowhere unless God led the way—I felt my fear about the future suddenly lift. I didn't have to face it alone. God was real and he cared about me. Instead of being depressed, I felt excited. Life had a purpose—my life had a purpose. I had ideas about where I was headed and how to get there. In the midst of my conversion I felt suddenly transported from midwinter darkness to midsummer light.

William D. Watley, pastor of St. James A.M.E. Church in Newark, New Jersey, captures the kind of transformation I am talking about:

> We usually think of stars as nighttime luminaries, but the morning star announces the beginning of a new day. Who can testify that "since I met Jesus, it's a new day now"? I used to be bound by the devil, but since I met Jesus, it's a new day now. I used to have low self-esteem and was in a constant self-destruct mode, but since I met Jesus, it's a new day now. I've put down my blues guitar and picked up a tambourine of praise. It's a new day now. People and things that used to upset me don't bother me anymore. It's a new day now. Fear that used to paralyze me and guilt that used to beat me up have lost their hold upon me. It's a new day now. Glory, glory hallelujah since I laid my burden down—it's a new day now.

It is a new day for anyone who belongs to Christ. We still have problems. We still struggle. But good stories never develop without conflict. The truth is that Christ has set us on a new course, infusing our lives with his light, his presence, and his purpose.

Join me today in hailing Jesus, our Bright Morning Star, the One who fills us with expectation for a day that will never end, when darkness and death will be words we barely remember. Together, let us lift up our hands, throw away our caution, and shout out aloud: "Glory, glory hallelujah! It's a new day now!"

Friday

Promises Associated with His Name

Some things never change. Imagine what bedtime must have been like a few thousand years ago. The children are snugly tucked into their corner of the cave. "Dad," a terrified voice cries out, "something's crawling up my leg!" "This bearskin is scratchy!" "Mom, she's hitting me. Make her stop!" And then the inevitable: "I'm thirsty. Can I have another drink of glog . . . pleeeease!" The chorus continues until their weary-to-the-bone cave parents finally assert their authority and everything is quiet but for the rustle of a few bat wings.

Little people always seem to resist the ending of the day. Come to think of it, I sometimes stay up way past my bedtime. Maybe the problem is a primeval fear of the darkness—we resist closing our eyes lest we will never open them again. I wonder, did human beings panic when they saw the sun go down for the very first time? Were they heartened by a brilliant white light hanging low in the western sky? If so, they were probably gazing at the evening star, which just so happens to be the second planet from the sun. Yes, Venus is both the morning and the evening star, a steady brightness that reminds us of the One who lights up our darkness and chases away our gloom.

Promises in Scripture

If I say, "Surely the darkness will hide me
and the light become night around me,"
even the darkness will not be dark to you;
the night will shine like the day,
for darkness is as light to you.

Psalm 139:11-12

In that day the deaf will hear the words of the scroll,
and out of gloom and darkness
the eyes of the blind will see.
Once more the humble will rejoice in the LORD;
the needy will rejoice in the Holy One of Israel.

Isaiah 29:18-19

Continued Prayer and Praise

Hold fast to Christ and he will give you the morning star. (Revelation 2:26–28)

Remember that Jesus is the radiance of God's glory. (Hebrews 1:3)

Be glad because Jesus shines on those living in darkness. (Luke 1:77–79)

Notes

Jesus the Savior

Page 46 Robert Farrar Capon, "The Lost Sheep and the Lost Coin," Program #4012, first aired December 29, 1996, posted on *www.30goodminutes.org/csec/sermon/capton_4012.htm.*

Page 49 The story of this hymn is told in greater detail by Kenneth Osbeck, *101 Hymn Stories* (Grand Rapids: Kregel, 1982). Posted at *www.webedelic.com/church/hailt.htm* (accessed September 14, 2005).

Page 50 Jim Cymbala, *Breakthrough Prayer* (Grand Rapids: Zondervan, 2003), 40–41.

Page 54 Carol Cymbala and Ann Spangler, *He's Been Faithful* (Grand Rapids: Zondervan, 2001), 15–16.

Page 55 Graham Kendrick, "Shine, Jesus, Shine," copyright © 1987 by Make Way Music (administered by Music Services in the Western Hemisphere). All rights reserved. Used by permission.

Immanuel

Page 75 Randall Frame, "Fixing Haiti," posted on the Power of Purpose Awards website, *www.templeton.org/powerof purpose/winners/summaries.html* (accessed November 21, 2005).

Bright Morning Star

Page 133 William D. Watley, *Exalting the Names of Jesus* (Valley Forge, PA: Judson, 2002), 94.

Praying the Names of Jesus

A Daily Guide

Ann Spangler,
Bestselling Author of
Praying the Names of God

Joy, peace, and power—these are only some of the gifts promised to those who trust in the name of the Lord. *Praying the Names of Jesus* will lead readers into a richer and more rewarding relationship with Christ by helping them to understand and to pray his names on a daily basis. They will also begin to see how each of his names holds within it a promise: to be our Teacher, Healer, Friend, and Lord—to be God-with-Us no matter the circumstances. Each week provides a unique devotional program designed for personal prayer and study or for use in small groups. In ways both surprising and profound this book reveals a rich portrait of Jesus that will move readers toward a deeper experience of his love and mercy.

Hardcover, Jacketed: 0-310-25345-4

Pick up a copy today at your favorite bookstore!

Fathers of the Bible

A Devotional

Robert Wolgemuth

When we take a Bible in our hands, we are actually holding a user's manual for fathers. Story after story, it reveals our heavenly Father's love for his Son—and for us. It also shares the accounts of earthly fathers whose examples we'll want to either imitate or avoid.

The twelve chapters in *Fathers of the Bible* offer slices from the biblical stories of men who were fathers. From them, we can learn something about the tasks, privileges, challenges, and failures of fatherhood. We'll discover the faithfulness of Noah, the conniving of Jacob, the unbridled passion of David, and the quiet confidence of Joseph, Jesus' earthly father. This book will help you ground your relationship with your children on God's Word.

Hardcover, Printed: 0-310-27238-6

Pick up a copy today at your favorite bookstore!

We want to hear from you. Please send your comments about this book to us in care of zreview@zondervan.com. Thank you.

ZONDERVAN.com/
AUTHORTRACKER
follow your favorite authors